Samuel Simmins

**A modern bee-farm and its economic management**

showing how bees may be cultivated as a means of livelihood

Samuel Simmins

**A modern bee-farm and its economic management**
*showing how bees may be cultivated as a means of livelihood*

ISBN/EAN: 9783337374501

Printed in Europe, USA, Canada, Australia, Japan

Cover: Foto ©Lupo / pixelio.de

More available books at **www.hansebooks.com**

A

# MODERN BEE-FARM

AND

## *Its Economic Management.*

———

SHOWING HOW BEES MAY BE CULTIVATED AS A MEANS OF
LIVELIHOOD; AS A HEALTH-GIVING PURSUIT; AND AS
A SOURCE OF RECREATION TO THE BUSY MAN.

PROFITS MADE CERTAIN BY GROWING CROPS YIELDING THE
MOST HONEY, HAVING ALSO OTHER USES; AND BY
JUDGMENT IN BREEDING A GOOD WORKING
STRAIN OF BEES.

BY

## SIMMINS,

*Author of " Direct Introduction of Queens"; "Simmins' Non-Swarming System";
&c., &c.*

———

LONDON:

WOODFORD FAWCETT & Co.,

112, FLEET STREET, E.C.

———

1893.

# PREFACE.

IN placing this work before the reader, it has been the Author's intention to adhere strictly to the Science of Practical Bee-keeping, and to refer to the natural history of Bees only in so far that the one cannot be separated from the other to secure correct management. Those wishing to study the complete Anatomy and Physiology of these wonderful little insects, cannot do better than secure the works of Cheshire, Cowan, or Cook.

With few exceptions, the instructions contained herein will be confined to the Author's own experience, which has extended over twenty years of close observation. The reader will therefore have the benefit of a lengthened and varied experience, and by following one recognized system, there will be little possibility of the novice being confused by the usual multiplicity of ideas upon any one subject. The exceptions will be such matters as have a very important bearing upon the management of Bees. When the beginner has mastered the present system he will then be in a position to use his own judgment in selecting the good and leaving out the errors of others.

The Author does not hesitate to say that he has himself learned more by his failures than by success, in that where he has failed there has been a direct incentive to overcome such difficulty; and as the result, some of the most important methods of management have been brought about, while time and labour-saving implements have been devised; all of which will be found invaluable to the Apiarist of the present day.

It has been the Author's utmost endeavour to place the management of Bees before the novice and those who wish to become Bee-keepers, in as clear and straightforward a manner as possible. He knows full well how difficult it is for one more advanced in the science to fully expose every detail of procedure, and how equally difficult it is for those just entering the ranks to grasp many of the details which go to make up the grand total of success; hence the reason why some apparently simple matters are gone into at length, that the learner may profit by the writer's own earlier experiences—in some cases, costly experiments and failures.

With regard to the foregoing it is to be hoped that those who are more advanced will not be wearied by that which is given for the benefit of others who have not much knowledge of the subject, remembering that we all have been in need of just such teaching. At the same time, the Author trusts the expert will find some things not before known to the bee-world, and which he will be willing to admit go far towards the economic production of honey; and, moreover, constitute the very "pith" of practical bee-keeping.

It will be asked: "What are the profits of Bee-keeping?" Many consider that there is a fortune in it, but this is not so. All may gain health and pleasure in following the study of this, the most remarkable creature in the insect world, but the number who make a profit out of this occupation will be limited to those only who have special qualifications, and are able to give the subject close study and application.

The man who finds himself adapted to the under-taking may safely invest his money, and be assured of obtaining, to say the least, better returns than very many other occupations offer at the present day.

# INTRODUCTION.

THE Culture of Bees is one of the most healthful occupations that can be named, and at the present day it is being adopted as a business, while the number of people in all ranks of life who keep only a few hives as a pleasant pastime is very large, as may be judged from the fact that the members of the various associations in this country make up a total of something like 10,000. Consequently, more honey being on offer, it has become much cheaper than it was a few years since, when the supply was very limited.

While an increased production has lowered the value, there is at the same time a larger and increasing demand for the bee-keeper's commodity ; and as he now has the benefit of improved appliances there is no difficulty in competing with present rates. In fact, it appears likely that very soon it will not pay foreign countries to send their honey here, as continued improvements are reducing the cost of production at home.

When honey was superseded by sugar, bee-keeping seems to have fallen into the background, but after a time light began to dawn, and some thirty years since, by using hives wherein all the combs could be removed separately at will, a great stimulus was given to both practical and scientific bee-keeping ; consequently, the ranks began to swell, as it became known that much larger harvests could be secured than by the old fixed-comb methods, and in every way the bees could be brought more under control. But more light was yet needed, and Bee Journals were established, but it was not until the year 1873 that this country could boast of one, and that was founded by Mr. C. N. Abbott, of Southall, who ably conducted it for about ten years, when it passed into the hands of the Rev. H. R. Peel. Soon after this paper was established we find Mr. Abbott inaugurating the British Bee-keepers' Association, his object being the diffusion of the knowledge of bee-keeping, especially among the poorer classes, as a means of bettering their condition.

In 1874 this body held its first great Exhibition of Bees, Hives, and Honey, at the Crystal Palace; and since that time other Associations have sprung up, one after the other, each holding its own Annual Show. Is it any wonder then that thousands have entered into the pursuit, and that many thousands more have become acquainted with the value of the busy bees' product.

The manufacture of hives and appliances has become quite an industry, giving employment to many; but it is generally carried on in connection with the making of foundation, as well as with some other, or all of the several, branches of apiary work.

Honey in the comb will ever remain a luxury, but that in the liquid form is destined ere long to be found in general use in almost every family, besides being used in various manufactures; and the apiarist should do his best to place the latter upon the market in as cheap a form as possible, at the same time being careful that such shall have a neat and attractive appearance.

# INTRODUCTION TO REVISED (1892) EDITION.

The flattering reception accorded to the first edition of this work, and the desire for a new issue, has encouraged me in now offering a second edition, after making a very careful revision ; while it will be found that much new and valuable information has been added.

The work stands almost alone in the peculiar position which it holds in relation to the honey-producer ; as it does not simply give the ordinary routine of management ; but enters particularly into the details of the more important questions of the disposal and current values of the bee-keeper's produce.

It is a matter for congratulation that the past year has seen a decided rise in the price of honey. Good extracted has been scarce, bringing as much as 8d. per lb., exactly the same rate (wholesale) at which I sold ten years ago. Comb honey has been eagerly sought after, but the supply being limited, the price at retail has actually been seen up to something like the old figure, viz. 1s. 6d. per lb., during the current winter.

I am aware of new individual enterprises being arranged for starting out extensively with the new season, in the honey producing line ; and there can not be a more favorable opportunity than the present, provided such endeavors are skilfully directed. The various honey companies which originated during the past few years have had to succumb, because the time has not yet arrived, and possibly never will do, when a single concern may carry out the business upon a scale sufficiently extensive to produce a dividend. Notwithstanding the failure of such companies, they have created a much larger demand for the beekeeper's produce, and a more extended knowledge of his industry ; though their action naturally brought about a too rapid decline in prices.

Nevertheless the total failure of the honey crop of 1888, followed by the very poor harvest of 1890, in connection with a succession of light yields in America, have at last convinced producers and dealers alike, that the hurried falling off in prices was premature, and not warranted by the current state of the industry. Instead of little more than sixpence per pound for comb, the apiarist can now hold out for ninepence to tenpence wholesale, and be sure of getting it.

It should be understood that small (less than 1lb.) packages for honey find little favor in general commerce. In every direction we see that prices are ruling lower than they were some ten years since ; and the consequence is that larger receptacles are required, so that jams and similar articles may be supplied to the public at the minimum of cost.

For rapid and convenient handling, the retail trade requires some protection for comb honey, but the producer must endeavor to give the best possible effect at the least expense, as he will certainly not be repaid for any great outlay in that direction.

A feature of serious importance to honey producers is the re-introducduction of the larger brood frame, much used before the present Association frame came into use ; the latter having repeatedly proved too small for the purpose, when its results have been compared with the advantages derived from the other.

My non-swarming system has been greatly improved, as by a new arrangement of sections, the worked out-comb may now be secured in them in the most perfect manner, while neither the foundation nor the combs are cut up to fit into the separate sections ; a great saving over any of the former plans of procedure.

The chapter on foul-brood will be found instructive, in that it conclusively shows how a cure can be effected by simple means ; and that the beekeeper of the future has no cause to dread the disease, because the rational methods recommended are the result of practical and successful application, and are perfectly sure in their action where only a moderate degree of intelligence is brought to bear upon the subject.

The Chapter relating to bees and fruit, seeding crops, etc., has been considerably extended, showing how largely the growers of such crops must depend upon fertilisation by the honey-bee in particular, for the success of their plans. It is a paper which should be largely circulated in the interests of both apiarist and agriculturist ; it will certainly result in a better understanding between those engaged in the respective pursuits.

The chapter on honey and its uses, has had some important additions made to it, in showing the practical uses of honey in both chest and throat complaints ; in what form to use it, as well as giving such recommendations for other rational treatment in connection therewith, which will seldom fail in affording speedy relief. This is a paper that should be spread broadcast by every beekeeper who has honey to sell.

The subjects of queen-introduction, queen-rearing, and many others will be found to have undergone careful revision ; while in some cases other valuable facts have been added, as the result of a further extended experience.

S. SIMMINS.

MAPASSA VILLA,

SEAFORD, SUSSEX.

# ILLUSTRATIONS.

# CONTENTS.

# BEE-CULTURE AS A PROFESSION,
## AND FOR RECREATION.

IT is now an undisputed fact that honey has become a staple article of commerce, and while it will be my intention to show that the honey-producing industry is capable of still greater extension in most of its branches, than has hitherto been the case, I hold out no golden promises, as too many are prone to do; but wish it to be distinctly understood that while the profits, under correct management, may be larger, the business requires more careful study and intense application than many others. A natural ability and a rational enthusiasm are necessary to make a successful beekeeper; and therefore, unless a man makes himself thoroughly acquainted with the peculiarities of bees, he is doomed to disappointment should he attempt to give his time and capital to this occupation.

There are two courses open to those who wish to follow the art of bee-keeping, whereby to gain a living, or for the purpose of adding to their present income. First, by having a few hives, and gradually increasing the number over a term of years, until the experience gained justifies one in making extensive additions to his working stock; though, unless under such very favorable circumstances as are sometimes found to exist, it will be unwise to discard any present occupation.

B

By far the better plan will be to

## Serve in some Established Apiary

for a couple of years, if possible. By so doing, you save time and money; your plans must be more definitely formed, and the solid experience thus gained will be far more certain to put you on the right road to successful management than half-a-dozen years spent in working up a small apiary. You start at once with all modern material; and buying in large quantities, a considerable reduction will be gained; whereas, many of the appliances collected from time to time, under the former condition of preparation, have become valueless by the time the apiarist enters more largely into the business, leaving out of the question that much of his material may consist of odd patterns, and cannot be used to the best advantage.

The man who has served his time in a large apiary will next have to consider how he is

## To obtain the necessary Materials.

In the first place, there is more risk in buying his bees than he is likely to incur at any future period of his experience. Many buy bees of irresponsible advertisers, and though the latter may consider there is nothing wrong with them, the purchase often turns out simply worthless.

If it can be so arranged, the student should by all means buy his stock from the apiary where he served his apprenticeship. He ought to know something about the condition of the same, and may rely upon the proprietor treating him honorably. Failing this, the owner will probably know where and how he can secure stock that can be relied upon.

Before commencing his own work, the apiarist will do well to visit all the apiaries in the country to which he can gain access, thus gleaning any valuable ideas that may be thrown out, while at the same time consolidating his own knowledge.

Under ordinary conditions there is a certain risk about bee-keeping; but the reader, by referring to the chapters relating to Planting and Breeding, will at once see how the whole thing can be rendered a certainty by those capable of following out the instructions to be found therein.

## The Choice of Location

is another matter requiring serious consideration. It would appear unnecessary to advise a bee-keeper not to establish an extensive stock in a district where an advanced apiarist already has many hives ; but he should not settle his bees close to a town, or near a public highway. Select some quiet spot, in a valley if possible, and the further from any manufactory the better, but do not lose free communication with some large centre, or railway convenience.

When you know that you will presently be entering into the business, have a good look around, and endeavour to secure a few acres in a district favorable to the undertaking ; a locality abounding in clovers, with the White or Dutch, in particular, as that most to be desired, and ensuring the highest average returns. Unless other conditions are exceedingly favorable, the absence of White Clover will result in indifferent returns, if not actual failure. This clover is sometimes grown as a crop, but more frequently the bee-keeper relies upon what is to be found in nearly all pastures, as well as by the road-sides, where the grit is very suitable to its growth. There is the Yellow Trefoil in May, also the Red Italian Clover ; and after the White has bloomed from the early part of June, as a crop, until near the middle of July in the pastures, there are the Limes in some places, yielding much nectar. The Sycamore, too, generally gives a quantity of honey ; then there are market gardens growing the various small fruits ; also large orchards, the honey from which, though not often large in quantity, is of considerable value to the bees while supplying the wants of a rapidly increasing population. It is seldom all the foregoing are to be found in the neighbourhood of Heather, though in Autumn it will pay well to move bees to the same if within a reasonable distance, as the honey generally commands a good price.

On chalk soil, particularly among the South Downs, we find the Sanfoin early in June and about the middle of August; Wild Thyme in July, and numerous wild flowers of the thistle family during the Autumn ; as well as a species of Trefoil (*Lotus Corniculatus*) during the Summer. Red Clover is also grown in great quantity, upon the second crops of which the foreign races only can work ; and as the first cutting of this plant would otherwise be very light, Yellow Trefoil is mixed with it, and this flowers freely for nearly a month before the first mowing. The blackberry must not be forgotten, in some parts being so abundant as to give quite a surplus of good colored honey; while the privet hedges are by no means to be despised.

Should the bee-keeper's lot fall upon any spot not so favorably situated, and expecting to work many stocks, he can only do so by making such arrangements as will allow him to

## Grow suitable Crops

which will also do for hay, and even in a good district he would do well to have some large crops going throughout the whole season. I have sometimes been asked

## What Amount of Capital should be Invested

to ensure a certain income ; but, considering I know nothing of the capabilities of those who apply by letter, it would be useless to attempt a satisfactory answer, and in many cases unwise to give any encouragement at all, where the fullest particulars as to locality and personal qualifications are not given. Everything relating to his surrounding honey-producing plants and trees should be well known to the advanced apiarist, who will not be certain of success on a large scale

just because a few particular colonies have yielded comparatively large weights. He will first find it his duty to pay the
greatest attention to securing the *highest possible average* return
from his stock, both by carefully breeding by a process of
selection, and systematic union of forces, that immense
populations may be on hand at the right time. He who has
thus far mastered the science, will have no need to ask the
foregoing question, but the list of estimated expenses may in
some cases aid enquirers to obtain the needed information.

It should be almost unnecessary to point out that "everything must be done at the right time;" there must be "a
place for everything, and everything should be in its place."
Thus by constant and careful attention, and by keeping all
things in order, the specialist will command success; but the
man who is not naturally of an orderly and temperate disposition, and moreover is not enthusiastic, and a lover of
Nature (the natural qualifications of a bee-keeper), had better
keep out of the business, or failure will surely be the result.
At the same time, it is by no means certain that reverses will
not occasionally be met with by the most expert and painstaking man; but such difficulties should be looked upon as
inducing a greater stimulus, with renewed effort and more
determination to overcome every obstacle.

## The Estimated Expenses for the First Two Years

will be found as under, the apiarist starting with not less than
100 colonies, and with some £500 as his capital; otherwise
he will struggle on for years before his business can be
satisfactorily established.

### First Year : General Expenses.

|  |  | £ | s. | d. |
|---|---|---|---|---|
| 100 stocks in " Standard " hives .. | ...at 30/0 | 150 | 0 | 0 |
| 100 extra body boxes, with frames | ...at 3/6 | 17 | 10 | 0 |
| 200 dry-feeding dummies ... . | ...at 1/0 | 10 | 0 | 0 |
| 50 rapid frame feeders ... .. | ...at 3/0 | 7 | 10 | 0 |

|  | £ | s. | d. |
|---|---|---|---|
| One 2-cwt. cylinder for reducing sugar to syrup... | 1 | 0 | 0 |
| Large glue pot, for melting wax to fix guides ... | 0 | 1 | 6 |
| Flat-blade scraper ... ... ... ... ... | 0 | 1 | 6 |
| Wax extractor ... ... ... ... ... | 0 | 17 | 6 |
| Timber for work-shop and honey-room ... ... | 20 | 0 | 0 |
| Labor ... ... ... ... ... ... ... | 10 | 0 | 0 |
| Timber for frame racks, store racks and sundries, labor, &c. ... ... ... ... ... | 10 | 0 | 0 |
| Rail carriage, cartage, &c. ... ... ... ... | 10 | 0 | 0 |
| Carpenter's bench and tools, nails, screws, paint, &c. ... ... ... ... ... | 11 | 10 | 0 |
| Rent (more or less) ... ... ... ... ... | 15 | 0 | 0 |
| Sugar ... ... ... ... ... | 5 | 0 | 0 |
| Total ... ... | £268 | 10 | 6 |

*Add the following if Comb Honey is to be worked for:*

|  | £ | s. | d. | £ | s. | d. |
|---|---|---|---|---|---|---|
| 300 sets of super crates, at 2/6 ... | 37 | 10 | 0 | | | |
| 6,000 1-lb. sections, at 22/6 ... ... | 6 | 15 | 0 | | | |
| 100 1½-doz. crates, glass two sides, at 2/6 ... ... ... ... | 12 | 10 | 0 | | | |
| 100 lbs. super foundation, at 2/6 ... | 12 | 10 | 0 | | | |
| General expenses ... ... | 268 | 10 | 6 | | | |
| Total, first year ... ... | | | | £337 | 15 | 6 |

*Add the following if Extracted Honey is desired:*

|  | £ | s. | d. |
|---|---|---|---|
| 300 extracting supers, at 2/6... | 37 | 10 | 0 |
| Uncapping stand, knives, &c. | 2 | 2 | 0 |
| Honey extractor ... ... | 1 | 15 | 0 |
| 6 honey cylinders, 500 lbs. each, at 15/- ... ... ... | 4 | 10 | 0 |
| 50 three-dozen crates, at 3/- ... | 7 | 10 | 0 |
| 25 one-dozen crates, at 2/- ... | 2 | 10 | 0 |

|  |  | £ | s. | d. |
|---|---|---|---|---|
| lbs. | 100 lbs. brood foundation, at 2/- | 10 | 0 | 0 |
| 1728 | 12 gross 1-lb. glass jars, at 14/- | 8 | 8 | 0 |
|  | 12 ,, corks, at 1/6... ... | 0 | 18 | 0 |
| 1728 | 6 ,, 2-lb. tins, at 18/- ... | 5 | 8 | 0 |
| 1296 | 3 ,, 3 ,, at 24/- ... | 3 | 12 | 0 |
| 864 | 1 ,, 6 ,, at 30/- ... | 1 | 10 | 0 |
|  | General expenses ... ... | 268 | 10 | 6 |
| 5616 |  |  |  |  |

Total, first year ... ... £354 3 6

### GENERAL EXPENSES, SECOND YEAR :

| Rent (more or less) ... ... | ...£15 | 0 | 0 |
|---|---|---|---|
| Sugar ... ... ... ... | ... 10 | 0 | 0 |
| Sundry expenses, carriage, &c. | ... 5 | 0 | 0 |

£30 0 0

#### *Working for Comb Honey :*

| Total first year... ... ... | ...£337 | 15 | 6 |
|---|---|---|---|
| 100 extra super crates, at 2/6... | ... 12 | 10 | 0 |
| 6000 1-lb. sections, at 22/6 ... | ... 6 | 15 | 0 |
| 50 1½-dozen crates, at 2/6 .. | ... 6 | 5 | 0 |
| 100 lbs. super foundation, at 2/6 | ... 12 | 10 | 0 |
| General expenses ... | ... 30 | 0 | 0 |

Total, second year ... £405 15 6

#### *Working for Extracted Honey :*

|  | Total first year ... ... | ...£354 | 3 | 6 |
|---|---|---|---|---|
|  | 50 3-dozen bottle crates, at 3/- | 7 | 10 | 0 |
| lbs. | 100 extracting supers, at 2/6.... | 12 | 10 | 0 |
| 2880 | 20 gross 1-lb. jars, at 14/- ... | 14 | 0 | 0 |
|  | 20 ,, corks, at 1/6.. ... | 1 | 10 | 0 |
| 1728 | 6 ,, 2-lb. tins, at 18/- ... | 5 | 8 | 0 |
| 1296 | 3 ,, 3 ,, at 24/- ... | 3 | 12 | 0 |
| 864 | 1 ,, 6 ,, at 30/- ... | 1 | 10 | 0 |
|  | General expenses ... ... | 30 | 0 | 0 |
| 6768 |  |  |  |  |

Total, second year ... £430 3 6

ESTIMATED RETURNS, AT A LOW AVERAGE, TAKING A SERIES OF YEARS.

*Comb Honey* : *First Year.*

|  | £ | s. | d. | £ | s. | d. |
|---|---|---|---|---|---|---|
| 100 stocks, at 30 lb. per hive—<br>3000 lbs., at 9d. ... ...£112 | 112 | 10 | 0 |  |  |  |
| Total for the year ... | | | | £112 | 10 | 0 |

*Second Year.*

|  | £ | s. | d. | £ | s. | d. |
|---|---|---|---|---|---|---|
| Increased to 125 stocks, at 30 lb. per hive—3750 lbs., at 9d. ... ...£140 | 140 | 12 | 6 |  |  |  |
| Increase to 150; sell 25 at 30/- ... | 37 | 10 | 0 |  |  |  |
| Total for the year ... | | | | £178 | 2 | 6 |

*Extracted Honey* : *First Year.*

|  | £ | s. | d. | £ | s. | d. |
|---|---|---|---|---|---|---|
| 100 stocks, at 50 lb. per hive—5000 lbs., at 7d. ... ...£145 | 145 | 16 | 8 |  |  |  |
| Wax ... ... ... ... | 2 | 0 | 0 |  |  |  |
| Total for the year ... | | | | £147 | 16 | 8 |

*Second Year.*

|  | £ | s. | d. | £ | s. | d. |
|---|---|---|---|---|---|---|
| Increased to 125 stocks, at 50 lb. per hive—6250 lbs. at 7d. ... ...£182 | 182 | 5 | 10 |  |  |  |
| Wax ... ... ... | 2 | 10 | 0 |  |  |  |
| Increase to 150; sell 25 at 30/- ... | 37 | 10 | 0 |  |  |  |
| Total for the year ... | | | | £222 | 5 | 10 |

The greater part of the expenses go towards stock-in-trade; but after the second year, the outlay will be smaller, while the returns will be considerably higher, as the apiarist consolidates his working force. The quantity of sugar required may amount to more or less according to the season, and the extent to which the bees are deprived of honey. The better management is that whereby the largest surplus is obtained *without depriving the stock-chamber* of honey at all; in which case the labour and expense involved in feeding will often be unnecessary. Having charged the cost of bottles and tins, the same is added to the selling price of the extracted honey, as showing the more correct estimate.

## Number of Colonies.

In reference to the foregoing estimates, it will be seen that it is proposed to keep the number of colonies but little over one hundred, increasing the first year to 125; the second season to 150. It is then understood that 25 stocks are to be sold; when the remaining 25 over and above the 100 will provide against all accidents, such as weak colonies, loss of queens, etc., during the winter; thus ensuring that the number shall not fall below 100. This is as far as any one person should attempt to extend until he is very certain he can manage more. With that number no assistance is required, but when greater extensions are decided upon, the apiarist should get some intelligent lad, and take care in teaching him to become an expert assistant. It is surprising how quickly a youngster takes to the various manipulations, and in this line he will, more often than not, be of more service than a man at much higher wages.

Where the apiarist is capable of making up most of his own appliances, his time will be mostly occupied during the winter, and then timber will stand in the place of many of the articles enumerated, making a considerable reduction in cost. The owner's labor in the apiary has, of course, not been estimated, as that can only be valued by the balance of profit shown at the end of the season : the laborer is worthy of his hire (profit.)

## The Average yields per Hive

for both comb and extracted honey, taking a series of years, have been placed very low, but in a fairly good district the beekeeper should have no trouble in exceeding those figures, if there are not more than a total of 150 colonies standing in his area, or range of bee-flight. In a very favourable locality, or where the owner plants bee-forage, the average will be still higher, and 200, or more, may be placed in one apiary without any apparent diminution in the "out-put" per hive.

The editor of the *British Bee Journal* states that he obtained 1360 lbs. from seven hives. This was extracted honey, but his results in comb have often exceeded 100 lbs. per hive. These weights were obtained from a limited number of stocks : it will be seldom, however, that such returns will be gained where a larger number are to be managed. I have had 50 lbs. stored by a single colony in seven days : and in 1886 had a queen sent me, whose bees, without attempting to swarm, had given upwards of 250 lbs. of honey, about 200 lbs. of which were in nicely-finished sections. Such results show what is possible if the apiarist will always breed from the best strains, as set forth in the chapter upon that subject.

## What Kind of Honey to Produce.

It has often been stated that it pays best to run an apiary for extracted honey, but my own opinion is that to obtain the most desirable crop, the apiarist should work for both that and comb honey. Certainly a larger quantity of extracted honey can be obtained, but this will stand in the proportion of 50 to 30 lbs. of comb. Most practical men will admit this is correct, and upon this basis I have made out the estimates. It will be noticed that there is little difference between the first cost on stock-in-trade, whether comb or extracted honey is worked for, but the season's produce of extracted honey costs for receptacles more than three times that of the other. After the combs are once established for extracting, with no further outlay in foundation, and a large quantity of new wax from the cappings, the balance may be in favour of this class of honey ; but against this we have to place more labour, and that not of the cleanest. I have published these estimates that the beekeeper may have a ready means of making his own comparisons, and be more certain of what he is about ; and I do not, by any means, intend the estimated returns to be taken as implying a certainty.

Dear reader, throughout these pages will be found my utmost desire to save you from the mistakes made in the past by myself and many others. Experience is of course the best teacher, and its lessons nearly always leave on record instances of failure, of a more or less serious nature, which has to be met before final success can be ensured. Experience thus gained is of value to others starting out upon the same course, just in proportion to their willingness to be guided by the advice given. Right here I must insist upon

## One Point of the Greatest Importance.

When you have decided to make a start upon a large scale, purchase your bees, in one lot if possible, about the middle of April, and have them removed to your own place at once. I do not contemplate that the transaction will take place at any other time, and can certainly give no advice for obtaining them at another date, where the highest possible returns are desired from the first season's work. If you begin earlier or later, earlier in particular, the first great mistake is made, and very likely one which will be the cause of ultimate failure.

## Bees moved in April

undergo just that condition of excitement which induces healthy activity at exactly the right time ; the queens become equally energetic under the consequent stimulation ; and better progress is made than if they had not been disturbed. If moved in February or March the same excitement causes the loss of thousands of the older bees, through flying for what they cannot obtain at that early date : the large patches of brood lose the warmth hitherto afforded by such workers, and

the hive deteriorates to such an extent that the whole season
is unprofitable.    By purchasing in April there are plenty of
young bees to fall back upon ; you get only good stocks which
have stood the ordeal of winter ; there is no further risk, and
the whole season is before you.    If obtained at a later date,
the first year is lost, and the excitement caused by later packing is not simply injurious, but absolutely ruinous.    These
statements are based upon hard facts and experience, and the
reader will do well to be guided thereby.

So far we have considered one branch of bee-keeping only,
but another thing is the

## Sale of Bees and Queens.

This is more profitable, more certain, and the returns quicker
than when producing honey ; but, at the same time, special
qualifications are necessary to enable a man to conduct
a queen-rearing business successfully, and unless he finds
himself peculiarly adapted to the undertaking, he had better
confine himself to honey, as continued application, constant
care and thought, are required in a much higher degree, to
enable one to carry on this interesting work.    It should also
be understood that where bees and queens are raised for sale,
the apiarist will have to be satisfied with but a limited
quantity of honey ; in fact, if his demand is large, in some
seasons instead of a surplus, a considerable amount of sugar
will be required for winter store, while his stock is seriously
handicapped during prolonged spells of bad weather, when
many virgin queens are on hand.    It will take some years to
gain a connection, and in the meantime your advertisements
must be frequent, but limited in extent and cost.

Do not attempt much in the way of selling bees and
queens until you have a substantial stock of at least one
hundred hives to draw upon, or you will never obtain much
benefit from them if you are depending largely upon this
source of income.

Still another department is connected with apiculture :

## The Manufacture of Appliances

is carried on by a number of reliable men, each of whom has
an apiary; some of them add the making of comb-foundation,
while nearly all find it necessary to continue some other
business.  On the other hand there are many, who gaining
a first insight into bee-keeping, think it a great chance
to make money by advertising hives for sale, either of
patterns already in hand, or some idea of their own.  This
branch of the business is now so much over-crowded, and
well-made goods can be obtained so cheaply, that there is no
demand for badly-constructed hives as the amateur often turns
out.  His advertising expenses are never returned, and, he
soon gives up in disgust.  I do not mean to imply that no
good is ever to be done in a small way ; but it is better for the
beginner who can turn out a decent article to confine himself
to local requirements, while continuing his usual occupation.
As a rule the buyer will find it to his advantage to go to
a well-known maker, and get what he wants at a cheaper
rate, and correctly made.

It is so far doubtful whether honey-producing alone, except
under particularly favorable conditions, will ever become a
reliable source of income ; but in connection with the manufacture of appliances and foundation, the sale of bees, etc.,
when well known, it is possible to secure good returns where
capital is judiciously invested, and labor is economised.
There are several rural occupations that can be carried on in
connection with bee-keeping to advantage.  Fruit-growing is
generally profitable to those who understand its culture.
Poultry, on a small scale, can be made most profitable, and a
large portion of the proceeds, in eggs and fowls, may find
their way to the owner's table, in addition to those sold.
Other pursuits may occur to the individual bee-keeper, such
as may not seriously interfere with the main occupation,

though his surroundings, and space at command, will largely
influence his actions.

## Bee-Keeping for Recreation.

While the greater number of amateurs endeavour to get all
the profit they can out of their bees, there are many who keep
them because of the pleasure afforded by studying their
habits; though, of course, the delight experienced in being
able to place pure honey, in its most chaste form, upon one's
own table, and that of friends, is by no means a secondary
consideration.    Nothing can be more appreciated than a
present of beautifully white honeycomb in sections or bell-
glasses; and what, moreover, can exceed the pride and
pleasure in thus being able to present that which is your own
production; a thing of beauty, which has been gradually
" growing " under your own fostering care.

The busy man who occasionally spends a few minutes
with his bees, finds healthful and soothing recreation for both
body and mind; and fortunate are those whose leisure gives
them almost unlimited time to carry out the study of these
remarkable insects.    It can truly be said that they are a
never-failing source of interest, there being always something
new to discover, either as to their habits or management.

Modern bee-keepers are enthusiasts, and among all who
study the subject there is a general understanding and mutual
sympathy.   The novice may therefore go to his nearest neighbor
who may be following the pursuit, and be certain of a hearty
welcome, and a free gift of all the knowledge about bees that he
may have gathered by many years of practice; but nevertheless, just here, I advise the beginner not to go to his more
expert neighbor every time a difficulty occurs.   He must bear
in mind his past lessons, and strive to help himself.

It does not much matter at what time of the year you may
begin in a small way; you have first to gain confidence in
handling bees before you can make much out of them.   Get

some friend or other apiarist of experience, if possible, to over-haul the stock you wish to purchase, and be guided by him as to its value. In the absence of friendly advice, you cannot do better than buy a first swarm from some cottage bee-keeper. Obtain your hives from a well-known maker, and so get them correct in measurement; otherwise your expected pleasure will be somewhat marred, and your manipulations sadly complicated.

While the number who may be capable of making bee-keeping their main occupation, will be limited, almost every-one can keep a few colonies at great advantage to health, and at the same time make them pay their own way. Even the scientist need not go to any great expense over his inves-tigations, as with ordinary care his bees can be made to return all the money he may require to lay out for such pur-poses.

The cry of "over-production" is but a false alarm, and we need not fear, however many become honey-producers in our generation. No genuine article of food will long want for a customer, if only it is presented in an attractive manner at a reasonable rate. There are many ways in which honey may be utilised, not only as food and medicine, but also for a num-ber of manufacturing purposes; and while the fact that many others will continue to enter into the occupation, may cause reduced prices, the value of honey will become more generally known, to the advantage of all concerned.

## CHAPTER II.

# HOW TO HANDLE BEES.

AMONG the uninitiated the general impression is that bees are certain to sting if molested, but if let alone they will not touch one. This is to a certain extent true, and while the novice would generally be unable to open a hive to take out the combs and bees, without being attacked, the expert may do almost anything with neither veil nor gloves, and seldom receive a sting. Of course, the difference is that the former has not yet gained that caution and confidence necessary in all his manipulations, and this will come only by practice; no one can give him the desired skill to start with. A calm and deliberate motion should be acquired by all who hope to handle bees successfully. I have known those looked upon as experts to have a very unpleasant manner while manipulating bees, making it unsafe for any unprotected companion, and disturbing a whole apiary for days. Though such operator may not himself mind stings, this carelessness should be overcome if the owners visited are to have any pleasure in their apiaries.

### Precaution against Robbing.

Where an expert is called upon to put an apiary in order, or remove the crop of honey, difficulties are likely to occur before he can get through a large number at one place, if precautions are not taken. As far as possible, while on a tour the larger apiary should be visited last, and the work so timed that it will be completed towards dusk, and no combs from the extractor should be returned until then. These remarks apply to Autumn in particular, though there are other periods when honey is not coming in, and not only then but at all times the owner should be very careful not to give his bees a chance even to *start* robbing, with its consequent fighting, loss, and annoyance.

Preventive measures are of course the first consideration, and in the case of fairly large apiaries some bee-proof shelter is a great necessity, as many operations may there be carried on which would be impossible in the open. Many of the stocks may be carried into such shelter for examination or deprivation; and besides being invaluable for extracting, will be found most useful for queen-rearing and many other purposes.

If through negligence in carelessly allowing honey or syrup to be exposed in the apiary, the

### Robbing Mania

has once commenced, as may also be induced by the injudicious opening of hives, or badly fitting floors, roofs, etc., then the uninitiated will find he has let loose a power which will require his coolest judgment to subdue it. I have known horses, chickens, dogs, and other animals severely attacked by bees because the skep of a neighbour having been placed upon an old block cracked in every direction, offered capital openings for a host of determined robbers, whom I found coming and going like some irresistible hurricane. All openings, except one reduced to a ½-inch tubular passage-way, were immediately stopped; the watering can was freely used, and dripping sacks left over the skep. In a few minutes all was quiet. Where the ire of bees has been aroused by the

c

careless removal of honey in Autumn similar difficulties are likely to occur, but in this case they will remain irritable for days or weeks.

Robbing in the same apiary is sometimes cured by making the attacked hive exchange places with that of the assailants ; carbolic acid in solution, on cloths placed about the front of the unfortunate hive, will put an end to the disturbance ; and where all the stocks in an apiary can be fed up simultaneously in the Autumn, there will be no further inclination to rob, and all the necessary work may be completed in comfort.

Having shown that the first care of the apiarist is to be cautious, that his bees may always be held well in hand, it will now be desirable to consider under what conditions they may be handled without fear of being stung. We will first note that as a rule,

## Clustering Swarms do not Sting.

Nearly everyone has noticed how readily a new swarm may be handled; the bees having no inclination to sting. The reason is not so much that they are full of honey, as is usual in swarming time, but that they are homeless, and have only recently been under great excitement. By the aid of some intimidant, the bees of an established colony may also be excited and made to fill themselves with honey, when the combs can be removed at will. It does not happen, however, that all the bees rush to the cells ; I have frequently noticed that many do not attempt to do so, but these may be already loaded, though the state of excitement is so soon communicated to all that none, as a rule, attempt to retaliate when the hive is examined,

When necessary to look into a fixed-comb hive (commonly called a "skep") first drive a few puffs of smoke in at the entrance from a bellows smoker, as illustrated, which is of the "Bingham" pattern. Give the sides of the hive several sharp raps, then turn it up in a line parallel with the combs, so that none may fall on one side, when, after a little more smoke driven across the now exposed combs, any necessary examination may be made ; though of course the investigation can be little more than a superficial one. The smoker is so arranged that when placed in a vertical position there is a continuous draught, but if put down the other way the draught is at once stopped, and the fire goes out. While it is desirable that no more be used than is really necessary, the operator should on no account proceed until he has used sufficient smoke or other intimidant, that he may be quite certain he has the bees well in hand. Many overlook just this necessary precaution, causing needless loss of bee-life, as well as inconvenience to others, if not to themselves. After any operation these little insects should, if carefully treated, be no more disposed to sting than before. Of course exceptions to this rule will be met with, and while at some more favorable seasons, and with some quieter races of bees, little or no smoke may be needed, there are other stocks nothing seems to thoroughly subdue ; and though these are often the best honey-gatherers, the novice will soon want to be rid of them : this is best done by deposing the queen, and giving one from a quieter strain. When it is desired

## To Drive and Transfer

bees from a straw skep, or other fixed combs, to movable frames, then after smoking and inverting the old hive, let its crown rest upon the ground ; place an empty skep or box above, fitting exactly mouth to mouth, and then continue to rap upon the sides of the lower hive with the hands or a stout stick ; but on no account jar in such a rough manner that the combs become broken from their attachments, or many of the inmates will be smothered in the honey. Soon the bees will be heard roaring on their march upwards, being in fear of the trembling combs falling about them. In the first instance a cloth may be secured around the junction of the two hives, thus ensuring that no bees rush out ; after a few minutes this can be removed, and the upper skep tilted from front to back, having first been secured to the other by a skewer, or anything that will keep them together without shifting. The operator will soon prefer to do' without the cloth and keep the skeps parted from the first, when the queen may be captured as she ascends, if desired. It should be so arranged that the back where the bees are to run up shall be the highest point, and that at the ends of the lines of combs, or the bees will not go up readily. Then transfer the combs to the frame hive, and return the bees, as explained in Chapter XI. One is often told to procure a pail or table whereon to place the skeps while driving, but if the operator will only bend his back he will want no such thing and will find the earth a far better "stand" than any other.

## Bumping.

After first intimidating the bees, another way to get them out, is to invert the hive and give it one or two sharp "bumps" on the ground, at the edge of the crown on the side parallel to the combs. If carefully done the combs break, away from the sides and top of the hive much cleaner than they can be taken out by any other way. Brush the bees off into an empty skep with a feather, and transfer the combs as desired. This plan was first introduced by Mr. F. Lyon, and has met with great success.

## Throwing.

This is quite an old plan, and where the combs are fixed, either by cross sticks through them in skeps, or in shallow-frame hives, nothing can exceed its simplicity and rapidity. Place an empty hive on a sheet upon the ground, mouth upwards ; stand over the same with the stocked hive held by the hands at the rim between the legs of the operator ; raise the hive and lower it quickly, then stop the motion with a sudden jerk just as the empty hive is neared ; repeat as often as necessary and the bees will be all thrown out. Wait a few minutes after smoking them, lift the hive and proceed, when the bees having discontinued feeding at the cells, will come out more readily. This rough and ready process was carried out only with the cross sticks through the hives and combs so that the latter could not fall ; and Mr. Heddon has more recently adopted the same thing with his shallow-fixed frames. In the case of frame hives the bees will be shaken down on the top, or at the entrance, of the lower hive.

### Manipulating Bees in Frame Hives.

The foregoing operations are seldom necessary with move-able-comb hives, as each frame may be removed at will, and this meets all requirements. When any operation has to be carried out, first lift the material covering the frames, and drive a few puffs of smoke among the bees, replace the "quilt," and after a few seconds peel the same off with care, and make the necessary examinations. Remove and replace each comb carefully, taking care not to crush any bees while so doing, and see that your smoker is on hand in good order, in case they may get troublesome. If the combs are to be cleared, shake them from the same back into the hive, or at the entrance by · a motion similar to that of throwing, beginning however with a gentle shake, and then more vigorously, as the bees become frightened. Nothing tends to subdue them so thoroughly, and on no account should a brush or feather be used until the bees have first been so shaken ; as by brushing them from the combs they are much irritated.

Carniolan and Cyprian Bees seldom require to be intimidated. The former can be handled almost anyhow, while with the others gentle treatment is necessary ; and what is remarkable with both these varieties, and also some stocks of Syrian bees, it matters not how long the hive may remain uncovered, they continue perfectly peaceful. With these, begin by peeling off the quilt gently, and then proceed to remove the combs in the same manner, and hardly a bee will take wing. Get them from the combs by shaking, as above, when necessary, and no stings will be given as a rule.

## Uniting.

Where bees are in fixed combs, drive both (or all), then remove all queens but the one wanted; stand the combed hive to receive them in an inverted position near to where they are to remain and throw all into the one. As soon as the bees are a little settled turn the skep right way up on two 1-inch sticks laid on the floor board; remove such sticks in the evening and see that the entrance is not less than 3 in. by ¾-in.

Bees in frame hives can be joined by alternating the combs of one with those of the other. Smoke each hive and then part the combs so that no bees hang from one to the other, and then proceed to unite the two. Leave only one queen, cover up carefully and do not disturb them again. If two standing near together are to be united, move the hive to be occupied half-way between the two, and take the other hive right away. A board placed against the entrance, slanting to the ground, will aid the bees in collecting at that spot, while the original inhabitants of the hive will also feel in a strange position. In general, when preparing for winter I nearly always wait until October and then a stock can be carried any distance in the same apiary and joined to another, with no loss of flying bees, as none get far from home at this date, and not flying frequently they always make a note of their position.

Many use thin syrup scented with peppermint wherewith the bees are sprayed, thinking that a common scent will make them unite peaceably, but there is no need of anything of the kind, if but one queen is allowed, and my directions are followed with regard to separating the combs and fully exposing the whole of the bees to the light for a few minutes before the union is accomplished.

Sprinkling with flour when uniting has recently been brought to notice through the columns of the Bee Journals; and the plan is certainly preferable to the above, and though I have no need for anything of the kind, there are many who will gain confidence by using it, though probably in the hands of a novice, careless handling will even then bring about a disaster occasionally. During the season I am daily uniting bees under all conditions without any extraneous aid, and always without fighting ; therefore to me the various recommendations are simply amusing.

In the case of Cyprians and Syrians some caution is needed, but I have found that if both lots are *first made queenless* these bees can be united without the least inclination to fight while in that condition ; the queen to be retained, being returned in the evening. Except it be in the middle of the day during a good flow of honey *nothing else* will induce these bees to amalgamate with strangers.

## Agents used in Quieting Bees.

Mr. Cheshire mentions that methyl salicylate, using a few drops on the hands, will effectually prevent bees attacking the same.* The same author also recommends a small amount of crude creosote placed upon the fuel in the smoker for subduing any colonies not amenable to milder treatment. The late Rev. George Raynor long used carbolic acid for quieting bees; his plan being to dip a feather in a weak solution of the acid and then pass it over the frames, when the bees rapidly retreat. Fume chambers added to bellows have also been introduced, and while I have no wish to disparage those who have invented these methods of applying carbolic acid, I am compelled to say that for general purposes I have found nothing to equal the smoker, and in extreme cases the creosote or other pungent article added to the fuel.

---

* " Bees and Bee-keeping," Vol. II.

## Gloves.

While I can but regard gloves as a great hindrance to manipulation, it is necessary that the novice should commence with something of the kind, just to give him confidence. Thick woollen gloves dipped in vinegar and water, wrung out, will answer better than anything, but as soon as possible these should be discarded.

## Veils.

These should be made of fine black netting to protect the face, while any white material will do for the back, and will protect the wearer from the heat of the sun. Elastic should be run round the top so that it will fit tightly about the hat ; and the length should be such as will enable the lower end to be tucked inside the coat collar.

## Sweetened Water for Quieting Bees.

In cases where very vicious bees have to be dealt with, or when a novice thinks he may be some time finding a queen, and particularly if he wish to hurry the operation of "driving," then first sprinkle the bees with a little sweetened water. After two or three minutes, all will be as harmless as flies.

## CHAPTER III.

# THE ECONOMY OF THE HIVE.

DESIRING to place a few important matters before the uninitiated reader in as simple a manner as possible, I will begin with the establishment of a new swarm, and explain the various phases of its existence until that in its turn is prepared to send forth its own increase.

Presuming that our swarm has been duly hived in moveable frames, each of which has a wax guide down the centre of the top bar, we shall find that the bees begin to extend themselves in festoons from the highest point should the hive not stand on the level ; if perfectly flat, then the cluster is formed near to one side, and forthwith waxen cells are added to the guide placed to ensure straight building. If the weather is favourable, the delicate white comb will be found to increase rapidly in semi-circular form, until the centre reaches to within ¼-inch of the lower rail of the frame, when the side spaces are soon filled in. Sometimes combs will be started in different places along the guide, and as the circular edge of each nears its neighbour, these are joined, and the several united continued as one comb.

By using a sheet of glass next above the frames, or better still, my glass rail sections, kept warm with woollen material, the interesting operation of comb-building may be watched. Many bees will be seen with strips of wax just removed from the " wax pockets " on the under-side of the abdomen, and this they are moulding into shape as added to the thick rim on the outer edge of the cells. This rim is always present, not only as a reserve of wax for lengthening the cells, but more especially for giving strength to the structure, and the better to withstand the tramp of many feet; the actual cell walls being as fine as tissue paper.  With a few exceptions, as when joining two combs, or where drone cells meet those of the worker size, each cell is hexagonal in shape, with a base composed of three irregular squares, so that the centre point of contact is deeper than the sides; thus, the centre of the base of one cell comes opposite the junction of three walls on the other side of the "septum."

The natural distance from the centre of one comb to that of the next is $1\frac{1}{2}$-inch.  It is not, however, absolutely necesary that this gauge should be retained, and it will be found by making the distance $1\frac{3}{8}$-inch or $1\frac{1}{4}$-inch when starting new combs that the bees will build them almost entirely of worker cells—five to an inch.  When the natural distance is allowed, many larger cells are constructed; these are for storage or for the production of drones or males, their measure being four to the inch.

As soon as the combs are sufficiently advanced, the queen deposits an egg in each available cell; this remains for two days, when the workers add a milky fluid; on the third day the egg hatches, and the tiny embryo floats in the liquid, to which the bees continually add, until the seventh day, when the larva surrounds itself with a silken web, its cell being then capped over with a porous mixture of wax and Pollen. According to Cheshire many more important changes then take place than hitherto have been supposed, and the student of nature will find much pleasure in perusing his work.* When fully developed, the insect bites its own way through the cap on the twentieth day after the egg was laid, and is readily distinguished by its light downy appearance.  It immediately proceeds to the open cells of honey, and helps itself liberally.  The youngster is generally assisted by an

* " Bees and Bee-keeping," Vol. I., Scientific.

FIG 1.

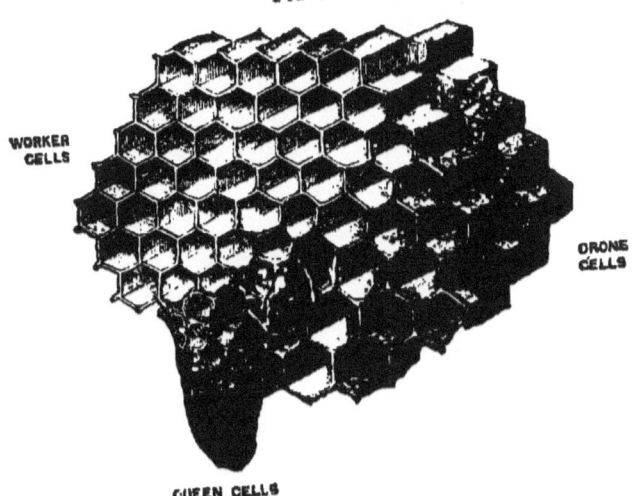

WORKER
CELLS

DRONE
CELLS

QUEEN CELLS

FIG 2.

WORKER

FIG. 3

QUEEN

FIG. 4.

DRONE

older bee in removing the filmy skin from its body, and after two or three days it goes out for a cleansing flight at the warmest part-of the day, at the time many others are having an airing and taking stock of their surroundings.

Our little friend gets stronger daily, and, soon after the seventh day we find her coming home with a lump of pollen on each back leg, in what are called the pollen-baskets, being hollow parts in the legs, with strong hair so overhanging that the load cannot fall. She enters the hive, travels up the comb to near the margin of the brood nest, and after finding a convenient cell, in which quite likely pollen has already been deposited, she pushes off her load with the middle legs, which Cheshire has shown have a peculiar instrument adapted to the purpose, and which is passed down the hollow behind the pollen, and thus it is forced off into the cell. The bee will then turn round and entering the cell, presses the pellets down into a thin layer, where probably many such are already placed, varying in colour according to the nature of the plant they may have been gathered from. It is well-known that the bee nearly always confines itself to one kind of flower when out foraging, hence its load of honey is of one kind only and the pollen is of one colour ; the bee-keeper may therefore frequently tell what his bees are working upon by carefully noting the colour being brought in. Thus mustard gives yellow pollen ; white clove, brown ; red clover, dark brown ; sanfoin, brown ; willow, yellow ; furze, dark orange ; dandelion, bright orange ; apple blossom, light yellow ; poppy, black ; blackberry, greenish white ; while the various garden flowers give every conceivable shade.

It is but seldom a bee gathers a large load of both pollen and honey on one and the same journey. A pollen gatherer will have little honey, while those carrying the most honey will seldom stay for a particle of pollen, more than what may be brushed into honey as collected. The pellets are brought in most freely up till 11 a.m. while everything is moist from the dew of night ; or at any time, immediately after a shower, if warm. The honey sources of the day are about dried up by three p.m., and the bees do not often work actively after that time. As in the early morning, they then carry in much water to help in preparing the food for the young, a mixture of pollen and honey, first digested by the nurse bees, or those not yet old enough for outside work, and given to the unsealed larvæ as a milky fluid. During the warm part of the day, not a bee will be found at the water fountain if there happen to be a heavy flow of honey ; but should there be a scarcity, many will be carrying water the whole day ; even if it be raining they continue their flights to the same spot by force of habit. It is, of course, understood that bees must have honey (or syrup), but, do not at any time lose sight of the fact that in building up in Spring, it is absolutely necessary that they have both *pollen* and *water* as well.

## Substitute for Pollen ; Water Supply, &c.

If there is any sign of scarcity, nitrogenous food can be given in the shape of a thick paste, formed by mixing pea-flour with good honey (syrup will not do). With a thin broad stick press this into the cells of a tough comb to the extent of half of one side and place the same next the cluster. Water can be given in large milk pans, either with sawdust at the bottom ; moss ; or wood to float as a resting place ; taking care that the vessel shall stand in a warm, sheltered spot.

## Young Bees take their Share of Work.

The honey gatherer will generally give up its load to the younger bees, returning at once to the fields, and it will be found that during the day the hives are filled almost exclusively with younger bees not yet able to work outside, and as these do most of the comb-building as well as store the honey, have we not here the reason why the pollen is so seldom found in new-stored combs ? Of course, we know that pollen is required near the brood nest, but much of it is purposely stored

and covered with honey in view of future requirements, and
the load could be transferred, as the honey is to the younger
bees, we should not be able to reckon upon the almost total
absence of that article from our comb honey.

That the young bees do take so large a share of the work,
as explained above, shows remarkable economy of labour, and
disproves the theory that there is no benefit to be derived
from brood hatched out less than three weeks previous to the
probable close of the honey harvest. During a heavy flow,
which implies, of course, very warm fine weather, I have seen
hives with none but newly-hatched bees at home, proving also
that upon an emergency young bees begin to carry much
earlier than is often supposed. The fact is, from the time
surplus receptacles are put on, the production of brood should
be limited to the capacity of nine "Standard" frames. That
number of combs crowded with brood, except for the usual
quantity of pollen stored, will represent the population needed
to make up for the continued wear and tear of bee-life, and to
keep the stock in good heart after the hard work is past ; as
few of those which have gathered the stores are to be found
within three weeks after the close of the season. Examine
the hive, and you will find every field worker has its wings
more or less worn ; look again, after the interval named, and
they are gone.

## How the Honey is Stored.

We will now watch a bee relieving itself of the nectar
brought in. Should she select an empty cell, she first assures
herself that it is quite clean, and then beginning at the base,
with her tongue she commences to "paint" the same with the
honey slowly leaving her tongue, until the first load completely
covers the three squares. Another load is brought, and the
next bee continues the operation of "painting" the sides of
the cell, but only so far as it is necessary to accommodate her
own load which she is slowly disgorging. In like manner

each following bee continues the process, until the cell is nearly full, and the mouth of the same is gradually sealed over with pure wax.   It will be readily understood that were it not for this process of moistening the sides of the cell, the honey would not always adhere to the dry surface, and hence much waste space would be the result.   Much of the honey does not, however, remain where first placed.   If the bees have room it is distributed as much as possible, and when the excess of moisture is evaporated it is carried above.

The bees which leave an air space just under the capping are Blacks, Carniolans, and some hybrids.   Ligurians give a thinner sealing and are not always so careful to retain the clear space, but their comb honey is quite presentable, though that of the former is preferred for its snowy whiteness. Cyprians, Syrians, and Palestines, however, leave no space whatever; in fact, it would appear that they even moisten the inside of the cappings, and fill the cell as tight as possible, hence their comb honey is not at all saleable.   The reader will therefore use his own judgment in the matter, and only work those stocks for comb honey that are known to produce the whitest comb surface.

As soon as the wants of the rapidly increasing brood nest are supplied stores begin to accumulate, and presently we find the upper portion of the central combs filled with honey and neatly capped, while one or more of the combs at one or both sides will often be a solid block of honey.   Meanwhile the population has been entirely renewed by the brood hatching in successive batches, but presently no more store is to be gathered, and then the drones are destroyed; the size of the brood nest is greatly diminished, until by September brood rearing ceases entirely, unless there be a queen of the current year, and in that case, with plenty of food on hand, it will be continued until late into October.   The whole of the stores accumulated by a swarm thus left to itself will seldom exceed 20 lbs., but let the reader compare this with the product of a swarm worked as explained under "General Management," and he will find that there is but poor economy in the "let-'em-alone" policy.

As the cool weather comes on, the bees which but lately appeared to fill the hive, crowd into a compact mass, occupying not one-tenth of the space. The winter cluster is formed where brood has lately been hatched, towards the central lower part of the combs ; thus the bees are able to enter these cells, head to head on opposite sides, as well as cluster between, forming one unbroken mass, and so keeping up the necessary temperature. In this state the bees do not rely upon any outside covering other than simple protection from direct draught. The older the combs are the more protection afforded in Winter; but one wall of the hive, at least, that on the south side, can hardly be too thin, as an occasional gleam of sunshine penetrates at once, and so enables the bees to shift their position, and re-arrange the stores around the cluster, even though the temperature may be too low for any to fly out. Therefore, wherever the entrance may be placed, it is absolutely necessary that the frames of comb shall stand end on to the south wall.

Providing pollen is at hand, breeding commences in all good colonies soon after the "turn of days," but at first the patches of brood are small, and limited to the very heart of the cluster, to guard against chill. It is not by any means to be supposed that henceforth young bees are brought forth without intermission ; but it is a fact, nevertheless, that a colony, failing through any cause, to produce this early batch of youngsters, will stand in the background all through the season, as presently the loss of bee-life will be so great that a late hatching of young ones cannot possibly keep pace with the deaths occasioned by almost daily flights. On the other hand, two or three generations of young bees brought to life before general flights occur, give a colony so great an advantage that no perceptible diminution occurs, and by the time spring opens, the population has been. *almost entirely renewed*, so that henceforth the progress of that stock is rapid.

D

Presuming that the colony we have had under consideration, has plenty of stores of both kinds, and a good queen at
its head, at the approach of May some of the large cells have
eggs deposited in them : these also hatch on the third day,
and the larvæ then undergo much the same process of change
as does the worker, though each condition is more prolonged,
and it is not until the 25th day that the perfect insect begins
to bite a way out from its cradle. Nearly every one has
heard of these burly fellows, but people generally appear to
consider that a drone is so called simply because he will
not work ; but the fact is he cannot work, and has nothing in
common with the worker, the latter being a neuter and its
whole organism so constituted as to fit it for work alone,
while the drone is exactly the reverse, and being the male
its sole occupation is that of fertilising the young queens
brought to life during the swarming season. It is therefore in
view of this colonising instinct that the drones are now
brought forward ; this being the first indication that a stock
is expecting to swarm at no distant date. If we suppress the
production of drones then, by allowing no drone comb, one
step is taken towards the prevention of swarming ; it being
well known that those colonies having few or no drones are
the least inclined to swarm.

## Royal Cells.

The next and more important step taken by the bees, is to
build special cells, either on the surface of the combs, or more
often around the edges, something in the shape of an acorn ;
indeed in their first stage, they are almost an exact counterpart
of the cup. They may remain in this state, as they often do,
for many days if the weather is not quite favourable ; but in
due course the queen deposits in each an egg, and as soon as
the tiny larvæ hatch from these they are fed excessively upon
what is called " Royal Jelly," a substance much thicker than
that given to the common larvæ. From the sixth to the

seventh day the developing insect has its cell capped over ; it then spins a cocoon which does not completely surround itself, as the abdomen is not covered, and strange though it may seem, it is just there that the cell is torn open, and the immature queen stung to death by the first hatched young queen, when the workers decide that the rest are not wanted.

On the sixteenth day from the laying of the egg, the perfect female, or mother bee, emerges from the cell, though she is not fulfilling her destiny, until being established at the head of the old colony or one or other of the after swarms, she mates with a drone when about six days old, and on the second day after begins to deposit eggs in the worker cells only. Contrary to the opinion of some writers, who affirm that a young queen is incapable of producing drones the first year, I have repeatedly had cases in *prosperous* colonies where a queen not two months old produced drones. Nevertheless, it is the rule for after swarms, having young queens, to build only worker cells the first season, hence no drones can be produced, and this would account for the erroneous conclusion arrived at by the old writers. Of course there is a lesson to be learnt at this point : " When wishing to obtain worker combs without the aid of comb foundation, insert young queens at the head of those stocks used for the purpose." But we have to note the

## Condition of a colony nearing the swarming point,

and therefore must return to the period when the queen cells are being capped over. The old queen now shows signs of restlessness and were she permitted would gladly destroy the inmates of the Royal cells, though only a few days previously she needed but little persuasion on the part of the workers to deposit the eggs in those very cells, soon to become her own rivals and deadly enemies of each other. It is not always the case, but it sometimes happens that the bees cease to stimulate the old queen to egg-laying at this stage, and hence she is better able to fly, as her ovaries are much reduced in size.

The bees have not always time to finish capping all the queen cells started ere the excitement culminates in the issue of the first swarm, the old queen coming with them, seldom first or last, but generally when half of the bees are on the wing. Bees of all ages come out, including those but just emerged from the cell. If the weather is warm, even these soon gain sufficient strength to fly and settle with the swarm ; otherwise, if they cannot crawl back to the hive, many will perish ; thus showing the necessity of a wide board reaching from the ground to the entrance, not only in this instance, but at all times, as many adult bees are lost in failing to reach the entrance during chilly weather. The workers out in the fields at the time of swarming and the large number of young hatching soon make up the strength of the hive and prevent the remaining brood getting chilled.

### Securing the Swarm.

If the apiary be located near high trees the swarms (if permitted to issue) will sometimes give trouble by clustering in them ; though they may as often settle upon any low shrub, or even a post or wall. In the former case a straw skep must be carried up and the bees shaken into it when inverted under the clustering mass ; descend the ladder as rapidly as possible, keeping the skep the same way, and then turn it the right way up on to a sheet previously spread upon the ground, with a brick or piece of wood under it, so that one edge of the hive may be raised to enable the flying bees to draw in. Where the cluster is formed on a wall or any other like place, brush the bees off into the skep with a wing; but if among branches of wall trees, little can be done in that way, and they must be driven up into the skep as it is fastened above them; by the use of smoke ; or, better still, make everything more certain by first capturing the queen and secure her in a cage fastened under the edge of the skep when placed on the ground : in this case if only a handful of bees can first be brushed into the skep, all the rest will follow. On no account, in any instance, expect the bees will go up of their own accord into a hive placed above the cluster ; it will only cause waste of time and disappointment ; it has to be done, therefore carry the thing through at once.

## Hatching of the Young Queens.

In about nine days from the issue of the first swarm, one of the young queens bites her way out of the cell, leaving the cap hanging attached at a part of its edge ; this covering will sometimes get back into its original place and be again sealed by the bees, and should a worker be in, clearing out the residue of food at the time, its fate is sealed in a double sense. Such occurrences, simple to a careful observer, have at times given rise to unfounded theories ; but at the same time it shows how it is quite possible to leave a useless queen cell in the hive when cutting out all but one to prevent after-swarming : a wanton waste of time, by the way, which cannot be tolerated in a modern apiary.

As a rule the first hatched young queen leads off, or rather goes with the second swarm ; though the after, and sometimes even the second swarm, is accompanied by more than one virgin queen. Though I am well aware that such queens will, if placed together, immediately fight until one receives its instantaneous death wound ; when several accompany a swarm, or in case two or more swarms settle together, each having a fertile queen, the bees themselves settle the matter by "balling" those not required. After the hive is so weakened that the bees know it is useless to attempt to swarm again, or should the weather be unfavourable, the queens still unborn are destroyed, as I have reason to believe, by the workers tearing open the side of the cells and there stinging their helpless victims, or tearing them out piecemeal.

Within seven days after the issue of the first swarm there are no more uncapped larvæ, and therefore no more feeding required from the nurse bees until the last remaining young queen is laying, a period of about twelve days, so that if excessive swarming is not indulged in, stores continue to accumulate while there is a reduced force to gather it.  It is well that this is so, as the young queen is generally so very prolific that unless the workers can get in advance of her requirements at the start, they are liable to reach Winter with no stores on hand.

I have here shown in a general way the natural condition of a swarm during one year of its existence, but under modern management the state of things will be much altered ; at the same time I hope the foregoing will enable the uninitiated reader the better to understand and follow such methods as will hereafter be described.

## CHAPTER IV.

# VARIETIES OF BEES.

### THEIR CHARACTER AND DISPOSITION.

I T will be my endeavour to give an impartial account of the different varieties as I have found them ; and while drawing attention to the great value of the foreign races for crossing with the bees we already have, I must advise the reader not to invest heavily in either of such varieties, but first obtain two or three queens and then compare them with those he already has for several years before making any radical change.

### THE BLACK, OR NATIVE BEES,

are still cultivated in many apiaries, principally because they are well adapted to the production of comb-honey. Their newly-stored combs are beautifully white, and therefore comb-honey produced by them commands a good sale. They are not so prolific as other races, and hence do not give as much surplus, and consequently are of little use in an apiary where increase is desired ; indeed, I can assert as a fact, the bee-keeper who expects to build up a large and prosperous apiary from black bees alone, will be certainly disappointed. When, however, he has all the stock he requires, no objection can be made to the sole use of this race where comb-honey alone is sought for.

Though, generally, the hives are less populous than those of other kinds, these bees have several valuable qualities. The young commence work outside at a much earlier age than the yellow races; they have great conservative energy, and a given number will produce and maintain a much larger amount of heat than the same number of any other race. Here is the sole reason why these bees are always more ready to take to the supers and are better comb-builders than others, though they may be occupying the same space with less than half the population. This I have observed for many years past with colonies standing side by side with the yellow races. For the same reason a Winter cluster of black bees is not so densely packed as one of the same size consisting of the yellow varieties. These remarkable peculiarities have not before been mentioned, and possibly never observed by other writers; but here is shown the very best of material for laying the foundation of a vastly improved strain of bees—starting with a race which has immense vitality; but requiring the ad-mixture of foreign blood to get (1) greater laying powers in the queens, (2) a better disposition, and (3) to eradicate their inclination to cease storing while honey is yet to be gathered towards the close of the season.

## To Perpetuate their Working Qualities

I have always found it necessary to breed from a queen of the native kind, crossing with Carniolan or yellow drone ; the act of crossing in itself adds greater energy ; while the disposition is received from the male side. For instance, a queen of a mild strain mating with a drone from a vicious colony I have noticed throws workers which almost invariably turn out to be irritable. Again, I have had queens produce workers that the average bee-keeper would not attempt to manipulate under any kind of intimidation ; and yet the daughters of such queens allowed to mate only with drones from stocks known to be easily handled, have given workers that one could do anything with.

I have found many black bees more irritable than any I have ever had, even rushing from the hive to attack a person many yards off; but by crossing the queens with Ligurian, or by preference, Cyprian or Carniolan drones, we get some of the finest and best tempered workers that can be desired. It has been considered that hybrids are very vicious, but this is only half true; what I have stated above is strictly in accordance with fact, but when any yellow queen is allowed to mate with a black drone, then, of course, the progeny resulting therefrom will be irritable, while their working qualities will be inferior to those of the cross recommended. Black drones are not required in breeding up a new strain, and should be rigorously excluded.

## LIGURIAN, OR ITALIAN ALP BEES.

These were the first yellow race introduced, and though much abused in some quarters, they have gradually gained ground until there is perhaps hardly a district where the native bees have not to some extent, more or less remote, received some benefit by the infusion of fresh blood. Indeed, it is amusing to hear some apiarists assert that Italians are inferior to the old-fashioned sort, and that they will have no more of them; when, as a matter of fact, their original stock has been greatly improved by the introduction of the foreigners, short though their existence may have been; and, moreover, the probability is great that year after year such short-sighted men are indebted to some distant bee-keeper for the continued excellence of their blacks (?); as the new blood is carried from one apiary to another, through successive stages during succeeding seasons; each cross showing less of colour, until in the end there is scarcely any evidence to show that the dark bees of the neighbourhood have foreign blood in their constitution.

The advantages claimed for Ligurians are as follows: They are more prolific, and consequently gather more honey

than blacks, more especially as they can work upon some
flowers not accessible to the others, and continue to gather
until Autumn is well advanced.   Strange to say, natives
often do best early in the season, but in Autumn I have
known Italians draw out foundation rapidly and store heavily,
while at the same time the former would not attempt to work
upon a sheet of foundation placed in the centre of the brood
nest.   The Italians are more gentle, and together with their
beautiful markings, this has done much to make them
popular.

They are considered to be an all-purposes bee, but their
comb-honey is not quite so good as that of the native kind :
they are not equal to the latter as comb-builders, and are
often hard to persuade to enter the supers ; while they are
unsuitable for queen-raising purposes, unless great care is
taken, as they will start but few cells.   A mixture of the two
races, however, as previously stated, will give energetic
workers, and there is no doubt that the " leather-coloured "
Ligurians mentioned by many Americans as being superior to
any, are nothing more nor less than hybrids.

As with all yellow races, Ligurian workers have three
yellow bands on the upper part of the abdomen, beginning at
the first segment.   Creamy white lines of hair follow the
broader yellow bars, down to the extremity of the body,
giving the bee a handsome appearance.   The queens vary in
colour from dark to light yellow ; while the drones sometimes
have patches of yellow on the abdomen, and others are hardly
to be distinguished from those of the black kind.

## CARNIOLANS.

Of all pure races, these are undoubtedly the best " all-
purposes " bees known.   Scarcely a fault can be found with
them, and while they are not quite such good honey gatherers
as Cyprians, the latter cannot compete with them for colour
of comb-honey.   It has been stated that they swarm im-

moderately, but this is more the result of bad management than a fault on the part of the bees.  There is one thing, however, which would give that impression : the demand for imported queens has been so great that I am afraid many old queens have been sent over, more especially as few of the native holders make any attempt to raise queens for the market.  Therefore, in the natural order of things, the old mothers would be superseded, and a number of swarms come forth headed by young queens.  Where old queens are avoided I am aware there is no more trouble with these bees in that direction than with any others.

They are so very prolific that considerable attention is required just at the critical time, in giving plenty of room, and free access to all parts of the hive.

One great point in their favour is their

## Good Temper.

Without smoke, or other intimidants, hive after hive can generally be opened, and no stings are received ; and without a doubt the introduction of this variety will do more to make bee-keeping popular than any device in hives which has been brought forward for the convenience of the novice.  Carniolans are *the* bees for beginners, and none need now start with any other kind.  By working with these, confidence will be rapidly gained, and presently, if desired, one may with greater assurance give other kinds a trial.

Carniolans are very active during the summer months, and yet are restful when confined during winter ; in fact, they come from a cold mountainous region, and there is, therefore, no doubt either as to their energy or good wintering qualities. It is reasonable to suppose that they at one time were a cross between Cyprians and the German bee ; the Cyprian element, however introduced, must have subsided, and the colour reverted to that of the majority, though the extremely broad white bands on the latter segments of the abdomen of the yellow race have been retained, thus distinguishing the Carniolans from blacks.

The above conclusions may be justified when it is stated that in crossing a Carniolan queen with a Cyprian drone, in most cases her bees are even more beautiful than Cyprian workers. In all cases the yellow element predominates, while few are less yellow than a nicely-marked Ligurian. On the other side, a Cyprian queen mated with a Carniolan drone does not throw a single dark worker. Again, I have had many hybrid crosses from a queen on the Cyprian side, after running through a few generations, each time with a black drone as the sire, when a bee resulted that could hardly be distinguished from the Carniolan of to-day.

The queens vary in colour from yellow to black: some being "ringed," the colour of the abdomen shading alternately from light to dark, but all produce workers of the typical sort, having on the abdomen near the thorax a mere shade of bronzed yellow, and then follow several extremely broad white bands, giving the bees an attractive appearance.

Many of the queens imported throw workers having one or two distinct bands of yellow, which show that the native bee-keepers have lately introduced some of the yellow kinds. This is unfortunate, though I find by careful selection at home that the typical race can be retained.

## CYPRIANS.

Among the yellow races these are destined to take the lead. Though not suitable for the production of comb-honey, they are very active honey gatherers and extremely docile, while their great beauty is undeniable. They have three bright yellow bands on the abdomen, followed by broad bars of light yellow hair. Unlike Ligurians, the yellow extends to the under-side of the body, as it does also in a less degree with Syrians. The body is much smaller than that of the native variety, tapering to a fine point, quite unlike the more rounded form of the other.

Some writers have given their experience as being very unfavourable with Cyprians, considering them vindictive and difficult to winter. They have faults, of course, such as being prone to develop fertile workers, and using much propolis; but all the stocks I have had could be handled at any time without intimidation; and as to wintering, the fault appears to be rather in the bee-keeper than the bees themselves. If the queen is not inserted into a colony too late in the season, and the stores are given at the proper time, these bees will winter not worse, but better than many others. When I say that I have had Cyprians hatched in August and September, continue in good health until the following June, it will be admitted that there is not much wrong with them; and this happened in the most protracted winter we have experienced for many years.

## SYRIANS.

These are, in appearance, much like the foregoing, though of a darker shade, and sometimes are not so well marked as Ligurians, though always yellow on the underside of the abdomen. Instead of having cream-coloured bands of hair like Cyprians, these have corresponding bars of a bluish white colour, much like the Albinos bred from an off-shoot of the Ligurian variety. While some condemn these as utterly unmanageable, others claim that they have many valuable qualities.

I have found among them queens producing workers almost unmanageable, while a larger number gave bees that could be handled like flies. How misleading, then, is it for persons who possessing only one—or perhaps two—queens, which upon throwing irritable workers, are induced to condemn the entire race, and thus prevent many from obtaining what would prove a really valuable acquisition. The whole matter resolves itself simply into this—select those of gentle disposition and breed only from such, destroying any queen which throws disagreeable bees.

## PALESTINES.

These are, perhaps, more yellow and beautiful than Cyprians, but can hardly be recommended, as they develop fertile workers to a greater extent, use more propolis than any others yet named, and while being handled have a very disagreeable habit of biting the fingers. These have often been confused with Syrians, but the two are quite distinct : Palestines come from the Holy Land proper, while the others are found farther north, in the Lebanon mountains. However, very successful results have been secured from a large apiary of these bees, in their native country, by Mr. Baldensperger, of Jaffa.

### Other Varieties

have been brought forward from time to time, including South African, Minorcan, and Punic or Tunisian. The first named are merely hybrids varying (in the same colony) from three yellow bands to almost black in colour, with the usual lighter bars of whitish hair between each segment of the body, in this case of a peculiar ashen-white colour. The queens are almost black, while the workers are smaller than those of any other race cultivated. A number of undesirable traits, apart from being hybrids, prevented their general introduction.

The Minorcans were freely offered for sale in this country, but these again, though similar to our native race, had no merits of sufficient value to claim the attention of practical beekeepers, and hence gained no favour.

The Tunisian is another of the darker varieties which, however, has recently come in for some notoriety, through some unexplained commendations accorded it by an advertiser in the Bee Journals. The race has been proved inferior to our native variety, and Mr. F. Benton, who first sent out queens of the kind from Tunis, has the following to say about them :—

" I always called them by the most natural name—Tunisian, and never thought best to strain after something a bit fanciful like " Punic." Perhaps the party who got up this name had in mind the ancient " Punic faith " in which this race resembles that of the old Carthaginians—for when you least expect it, *i.e.*, when they have been well, and even royally treated, they will sally out and cover the manipulator with their tiny javelins. They carry in more propolis than any other race, and are poor winterers. I handled several hundred colonies two different seasons in Tunis; took some to the Orient with me, also had them tested in Palestine, and I tried them in Munich, and came to the conclusion that in no way do they excel Cyprians, and in some points they are behind that race; would therefore advise to let Tunisian (Punic bees) quite alone."

CHAPTER V.

# HOW TO OBTAIN GOOD WORKING STOCK.

IN all apiaries it is found that a certain colony, or perhaps a few stocks, surpass all the rest in the amount of honey collected; and the remark is often made that of two colonies standing side by side, apparently equal in every respect, one gave a large surplus while the other did almost nothing. Reader, let us reason together, and see if it be not possible to explain the apparent mystery. As a matter of fact

### The Whole Secret of Successful Honey Production

consists in always maintaining the proper proportion of adult working bees in relation to the quantity of brood and young bees on hand. Here, then, can be discerned the difference. One colony was so favourably constituted that the queen was able to produce the full working force *before* the honey flow came on; while the other could not breed to her fullest capacity until *after* the season commenced. In the latter case the working force is unable to do much more than keep the rapidly increasing brood nest and large population of young bees supplied. With such an undue proportion of consumers on hand the queen now has it all her own way, and her combs are one mass of brood.

The colony which gained the proper balance of population at an early date, on the contary, has much reduced its brood nest by storing some honey and large quantities of pollen. This is the hive which will give the heavy surplus, and the other can never compete with it, even though it has twice the population. Of course excessive breeding can be to a certain extent modified by contracting the size of the brood nest, but nevertheless the actual working force will not be in excess until the season is far advanced.

We must now consider the causes of such a wide difference. They are many, one of the first being that the queen may be stimulated to breed too late in the autumn ; consequently she will be late to begin breeding the following season. The hive may have been short of stores, or the combs so overloaded in early spring that there is really no chance for the bees to develop the brood nest. Perhaps they were thrown back by being too much exposed, instead of having warm material above them. In either case an early hatching of young bees would be out of the question ; and these are the mainstay, compensating for the loss of many veterans when frequent flights become necessary. Consequently the best powers of the queen are not expended before the season opens.

## To obtain good Stock,

it is absolutely necessary that one keep only the very best queens—young, highly prolific and well developed. When I mention young, I mean just what I say. How wasteful and unnecessary ! you say ; but I assert as a fact that to enable one to keep his stock *generally* in the highest state of efficiency, he must retain no queens that have seen their second summer. Take a queen raised even so late as August ; she will be in full profit the following season : keep her till another season and her colony will be hardly second-rate.

To be prolific a queen must not simply keep pace with her workers while building up in preparation for the season, but must actually force them to make room for her. Such queens are to be had, and with them no "brood spreading" by the

E

apiarist is necessary. A well-developed queen is more hardy and energetic than a smaller one; and, as a rule, will get mated in risky weather when twenty inferior queens fail to meet a drone.

The finest queens are obtained from young mothers. A queen is in her highest state of excellence soon after she commences to lay, and can be used for breeding other queens, if from stock of known excellence, as soon as it is found by her hatching bees that she has mated correctly.

## Queens cannot be too Prolific.

I am aware that there are some bee-keepers who consider that a queen can be too prolific. It may be so with their management, but as a simple matter of fact the more prolific the queen, the larger the surplus stored, *but* one's management must provide that she does her best before the season opens; thereafter she will simply keep pace with the wear and tear upon the life of the workers.

It will be asked, "And how are we to provide that the best powers of the queen are to be used up before actual storage commences?" Some important matters having reference thereto I have already given; but one way of doing this is to unite two or more colonies, making them very strong in the Autumn whenever it is found stocks are at all under full strength. Another plan is to unite about ten days before the season is expected to open and thus in either case providing that the number of actual gatherers shall presently be far in excess of those required to attend to the young.

As a rule, especially where no honey is obtained after July, the best results are secured by preventing the issue of swarms; but nevertheless, unless

## The Equivalent of Swarming

is allowed our stock must deteriorate as a natural consequence. Therefore select one out of every ten colonies and devote it to queen-raising (see chapter on same), and allow one nucleus with a young queen to stand by the side of every stock. By the Autumn such nuclei will have themselves become fairly strong, when the old queens can be destroyed and the two lots respectively united in the evening of the following day.

Having studied the general rules to be observed if we wish to have only good working stock, we must now consider which are the

## Most Suitable Bees

for our purpose, whether we intend to work them for comb or extracted honey.

The advantages to be derived from the foreign varieties can hardly be over-estimated, for by crossing with queens of the native kind, we get greater fecundity, and better honey-gathering powers than either pure race possesses. In a former chapter I have already shown that a black queen must form the basis from which to build the very best working strain. Select such queen of known excellence and for the production of comb-honey use Carniolan drones to mate with young ones raised from her ; the first cross being the most suitable.

For extracted honey the second cross to Cyprian drones will be found to give the best results. Pure black bees are not at all desirable for either purpose, as they cease storing quite a month sooner than the foreign varieties or hybrids ; moreover, they are frequently troubled with the wax moth, while the latter never are. Pure Cyprians, Carniolans, Syrians, and Ligurians, in the order named, are also suitable for producing extracted honey.

Let it be observed that black (native) drones are to be rigorously excluded, as these give bad-tempered workers when crossed with a queen of either of the foreign varieties. Syrian drones also should not be allowed, though queens of that variety crossed with Carniolan drones produce excellent bees.

In concluding this chapter, I must insist that unrestricted
or indiscriminate swarming, as hitherto generally practised,
*is totally at variance with all true principles of breeding.* To obtain
the best results, it is absolutely necessary that all queens be
carefully bred from the best stock only. Our motto should
be " Excelsior ! "

## CHAPTER VI.

# PLANTING FOR BEES.

H AVING shown how to secure good stocks, the next thing is to provide employment for such vast populations throughout the summer. In the best of localities there is always some interval when nothing of importance is in flower, while many districts are so poor in honey-producing plants as to be quite unsuitable for carrying on bee-keeping extensively. Judicious planting, therefore, should make the culture of bees a safe and reliable investment, as the crops will be *near at home*, and always ready for the bees, whenever the weather is favourable for the secretion of honey. Indeed, with "a sea of bloom" close at hand, a surplus often accumulates during dull weather, when otherwise the stores of the hive would be diminishing.

Do not think of planting mere patches of various kinds of flowers; such are but a "drop in the ocean," and if you cannot provide more than a few acres, then put in some one thing that will come in as a main crop, if your district is short of bee forage; such as White or Alsike Clover, the latter by preference. If your surroundings are fairly good, then let the crop be arranged to come right for a time of scarcity.

### Area required for 100 Colonies.

You may be able to spare many acres for a continual supply, and in that case provide not less than 20 acres for each succeeding crop to every 100 colonies. I have by actual experience found 100 average colonies store a surplus from 10 acres of an average yielding plant, and should consider 20 or 25 acres would give full occupation at each time the crop is flowering, for that number of stocks with which to commence the season. But we have to prepare for the whole season, say from June 1st to September 1st; and, providing we plant such crops as will flower twice in the same year, we shall require in all at least 75 acres per year for each 100 colonies, in addition to the usual resources of the district. Without considering the latter, we have then, at the lowest estimate, allowing for bad weather at times, a return of something like £200 worth of honey for the 75 acres; it being considered that Clover, Sanfoin, &c., produce 10 lbs. of honey per acre each fine day.

A crop of this kind remains in its prime about fourteen days, so without considering the time " coming on " and " going off"; this estimate is based upon only seven days' gathering of five pounds per acre upon each first and second crop.

It should be remembered that the honey is obtained at no expense to the crop of hay, unless the same be allowed to stand too long before being mown. Even for the sake of the bees, most crops should not stand until the greater part of the heads die off, as such ripening process destroys the chance of a second crop. As a rule, those

## Plants should be Grown that are Useful for Hay,

after the bees have had their gathering. There are only two kinds that I can recommend for bees which are scarcely suitable for cattle, and those are Melilot clover (*Melilotus alba*) and Borage. There may be many others that give much honey, but there is this about them—they require constant care and attention to keep the ground clean, therefore for honey alone such plants are quite out of the question. The two named, however, can take care of themselves; they outgrow everything else, yield large quantities of the best of honey, and require only that the ground be turned or ploughed, in the case of Borage every winter, and the other each alternate winter. The latter flowering only in its second year, two or more layings must be provided to maintain a succession. Borage comes best with the ground turned up roughly and needs no further care ; but Melilot requires that the earth be harrowed and then rolled as often as possible whenever the surface is dry. Do not neglect to roll again the second year, both before and after the leaf begins to show. The omission of this very important matter is why the crop fails with many. We are sometimes told that this plant does well on poor ground ; I have had it on both that and rich land, with the advantage of three to one in favour of the latter.

## For a Succession,

the following will be found most serviceable. Italian crimson clover (*Trifolium incarnatum*) is an excellent honey plant used for early greenmeat, flowering generally in May, but can be sown to give a good succession. White or Dutch clover would follow at 15th of June till first week of July. Alsike cut for greenmeat just before it would flower will then, in its second growth, follow white, which will keep up the succession till Melilot is in full flower at end of July, the latter remaining in bloom as late as desirable.

## Late Forage Undesirable.

While we can hardly plant anything that will come in too early, it must be distinctly understood that nothing should entice the bees to work one day later than the 15th of September. Therefore if you have Melilot or any other large crop flowering at that date, do not delay, but cut it down. Bees need at least six weeks to regain lost numbers after winter is past ; they require just as much time to settle down quietly before the cold season comes on.

## Cultivation.

It will be understood that most of the above clover crops, etc., are sown over corn in the spring, the plant being well established by the time the same is harvested, and having the ground all to itself the second year. As to manure, that question is left to the reader to feed his crops as he will, remembering that what is worth doing at all is worth doing well.

Sanfoin is an excellent plant on chalk soils, giving two crops yearly, as also will several of the clovers if treated liberally. The former is allowed to remain from two to ten or twelve years, according to the nature or cleanliness of the ground ; when brought under cultivation, a second sowing will be of no avail until after a period of fourteen years. Red clover (*Trifolium pratense*) is nearly always ploughed in after the one full season's growth, and does not follow on the same ground again until after a term of seven years. Yellow trefoil or hop clover, should be mixed with clover and sanfoin to make a good first crop. After the first mowing the trefoil does not again appear, but the main crop then branches out and fully covers the ground.

I have found that for all small seeds such as clovers, the ground should be finely pulverised and rolled before the seed is sown. Do not rake or harrow after it is in, but use the roller again and again, when the ground is dry.

Whatever may have been said in the past, it must be distinctly understood that Red Clover (*Trifolium pratense*) is *not* a reliable bee plant. I have had considerable honey from it when the weather has been just right, following a dry time for the growth of the second crop, but should the plant have a favourable season for full development, the bees do nothing upon it however fine the weather may be. A crop yielding only one year in four cannot be recommended.

When growing plants for honey which have no further use, one must make the most of the land under cultivation. To permit the ground to be occupied by a single variety taking two years to arrive at maturity is sheer folly : and even with those flowering yearly something else must be growing at the same time.   Thus in preparing for Melilot clover, put in borage seed at the same season, the latter flowering the first year.   Mow the whole in July when the clover is getting rather long, and a second crop of borage will come on, while the clover will shoot out stronger.   Cut all again in September, and if harvested or used as ensilage, some use will be found for the mixture as fodder.   The second year, however, the Melilot will be useless for feeding after it has blown, and the growth will have been so rapid that little borage will be seen ; but the latter will again come up quite thickly the third year, to be cut twice as before with the new Melilot plants.

Again, when white clover is put down for bees, the ground can be filled with crocus bulbs, planted about six inches apart. They thrive exceedingly well, and being very early, will be found useful without in any way interfering with the clover, which can be mown with the crocus grass in July, when a second crop of clover follows ; thus we have three bee crops yearly on the same ground, without further cultivation ; the second crop of clover being allowed to seed the ground.   The white clover is particularly partial to road grit, and where the sidings, &c., can be secured, they will be found the most valuable fertilizer that can be obtained for the crop ; often inducing a heavy growth where the plant was seldom seen previously.   A great advantage to be gained from continuous bloom is that the surplus may be removed at any time without exciting the bees to rob, as is too frequently the case when the later harvest is taken at a time they have nothing more to keep them employed.

### Systematic Planting makes Profits Certain.

This branch of apiculture has been much neglected, but bee-keeping as a profession can only become a certainty in this country where systematic planting is carried out.   Indeed, even in America the same statement would apply to most

districts, as there is a frequent occurrence of poor honey
seasons, whereas with heavy crops close at home it could be
so arranged that a good surplus would be obtained *every*
year, though with scattered crops it sometimes happens that
the bees store little or nothing.

No one has done so much in America to encourage the
planting of bee-forage near the apiary as Mr. T. G. Newman,
editor of the *American Bee Journal*. He not only recommends
it as being an advantage, but has always *insisted* that it is
*absolutely necessary*, and one of the first duties the bee-keeper
owes himself. I quote the following from Mr. Newman's
*Bees and Honey* :—" In view of the uncertainty of nature providing sufficient continuous bloom, and the certainty of
annually recurring periods of cold weather, and long hazardous
confinement, the bee-keeper, to ensure success, should as
conscientiously provide pasture from which his bees can
gather food, as to provide hives with which to shelter them
from the storms. *With a liberal allowance of good, wholesome
honey in the fall, the first requirement for successful wintering will
be provided.*" 

Observe the last sentence ; what a world of meaning the
words convey to those American and other bee-keepers who
so often lose heavily during winter ! Our cousins across the
water put their losses down to bacteria, pollen, cold, etc. ; but
their late-gathered honey is not always good and wholesome,
while in many cases, if it is good, it is gathered often so late
as October. Thus the vitality of the bees is undermined too
late for recuperation by breeding before the cold of winter is
upon them. Nothing is so exhaustive as the gathering and
storage of a heavy surplus, and thus the too late gathering
places a colony at a tremendous discount for wintering.

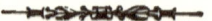

## CHAPTER VII.

# THE AGRICULTURIST AND FRUIT GROWER.

THE value of crops suitable for bee-forage has been shown by the preceding chapter. The bee-keeper who is also a farmer therefore has every advantage and can make profit in several ways. But while it is necessary that the extensive bee-keeper should also be a farmer, it is quite as important that the agriculturist should keep a few stocks for the sole purpose of fertilising the clover and other crops he may save for seed, if it happen that few bees are cultivated in his neighbourhood.

It should be distinctly understood that the more bees that can be obtained as fertilising agents, the more seed will be perfected, as well as more fruit. Single hives have been placed in cucumber and peach houses, and though some bees are of course lost in the first instance, the younger portion of the population never having flown outside, have no difficulty in finding their way about. The results have been reported to be most satisfactory, and the plan should be more extensively adopted.

Strange as it may appear to those who are inclined to grumble at the visits of the bees to their fields or gardens, it is a simple matter of fact that if the honey be not gathered it will only evaporate, and none is secreted after the flower begins to fade.

Fruit growers often complain that the bees damage their crops, and in autumn, when there is nothing else to be obtained, because they see a few bees among the wasps and flies, the former get all the blame; whereas they have never been known to break through the skin of sound ripe fruit, but simply lick up the moisture that may be present where birds, wasps or other insects have first made an inroad.

## Fruit Culture

for the purpose of jam making is now making such rapid head-way in this country, that all growers should have the subject of bee-culture brought very forcibly before their notice. The presence of a few hives in the immediate vicinity of fruit gardens and orchards is not simply a benefit to the grower, but is a matter of the first importance; and those who wish to secure the nearest approach to constantly recurring profitable crops, will find it an absolute necessity to encourage the presence of the domesticated honey bee. In some instances at least, particularly with farm crops, there is simply the loss of seed where the flowers had escaped fertilisation, but in far too many cases where the blossom is not fully fertilised by the agency of the bees, the fruit is not only imperfectly developed but in many places does not develop at all. In my own experience, which is also substantiated by other similar reports, it has been remarkable to find in my bee garden a full, and sometimes an abundant crop of fruit, while the general reports have told of failure and scarcity.

In a neighbourhood where many bees are cultivated, and more particularly in the garden they may occupy, it is very rarely, indeed, a poor crop of fruit is found; simply because the bloom is so thoroughly and regularly fertilised by the action of the bees, in securing a constant transmission, and mingling of the pollen.

The failure of fruit crops has repeatedly been put down to the devastating action of various moths, and other possible and impossible causes; but while the ruin thus created is very frequently only imaginary, the absence of suitable insect fertilisers is a deplorably frequent and only too noticeable occurrence.

It is plainly evident that the fruit grower of the future who attempts to conduct his business without taking every means to secure the aid of the industrious honey bee will be like a captain attempting to carry his ship through the seas without a rudder. More or less success has of course been obtained in the culture of fruit in the past; but the growers have not hitherto had their eyes fully opened, that they could tell why the greater success, or the least profitable result, and even loss, should occur. The proximity of a larger or smaller number of hives will generally be found to sufficiently explain the variations. The state of the weather, and all supposed enemies of the fruit gardens, will receive far less consideration when the foregoing remarks are fully appreciated and acted upon. A single hive, or even a dozen, will be of little use where there are large gardens and orchards. From twenty-five to one hundred stocks will be needed to secure the best possible results, according to the extent of the fruit farm ; and even if no one on the premises understands the management of bees, after defraying the expense of employing an expert either occasionally, or permanently where the number nears one hundred, there will be a considerable profit on an apiary so favorably situated, while the immense benefit conferred upon the fruit crops will be entirely gratuitous.

Any neighbouring bee-keeper should be encouraged, and in many cases expense may be saved by arranging with such apiarist to place a few of his hives in some sheltered spot on the premises, where the bees will be close at hand during the critical period of fruit bloom.

## CHAPTER VIII.

# ENEMIES AND DISEASES OF BEES.

A LONG list is frequently given under this head, but, so far as I am aware, if all colonies are strong, there is not a single enemy that can make any impression upon our stocks ; and as to birds, the injury caused by them is more fanciful than real. They do occasionally take bees, but according to my own observation it is seldom anything but drones and dead workers that are consumed.

Of the diseases, too, there is but one which requires any serious consideration, and that is

### FOUL BROOD,

so called until lately, but now designated *Bacillus Alvei* by Mr. Cheshire, who has made most exhaustive experiments and investigations in regard to this matter, and now tells us that the disease affects not only the brood, but the adult bees, and queen as well.

It has so frequently been stated that the disease can be discovered by the foul smell emitted by the stock which may have it, that I consider it necessary to warn the uninitiated not to wait for such a rude awakening. At that stage it is very infectious indeed, and it will be a saving to burn the hive and contents at once. With a colony in such a state the novice is certain to do only harm by attempting a cure, and it is well to be clear of it.

The disease is first to be noticed by the unsealed larvæ turning yellow, and then dark brown or black, instead of ever presenting a pearly white appearance, while some of the capped brood is in the same state, with coverings pierced and sunken. Now, here is a distinction to be observed between the genuine foul brood and simple chilled or dead brood. In the former case none of the larvæ dries up to a white cinder, being always rotten and slimy, so that the bees do not, as a rule, remove it from the cells.

### Chilled Brood and Simple Dead Brood.

The former is soon removed by the bees, and should any be overlooked, it dries into a hard lump without changing colour. Simple dead brood resulting without chill, and with no apparent evidence of disease, has in some cells the appearance of the genuine foul brood, but with this the greater part of the nearly mature bees dry up and retain their original form and colour. By this feature alone 1 have always been able to distinguish the difference between the two, and have put an end to the more simple affair in all cases by destroying the queen and giving a young and vigorous one to the colony.

### Cheshire Cure for Foul Brood.

Mr. Cheshire has presented to the bee-keeping world what has in his own hands cured some of the worst cases of foul brood that he could secure. The remedy is absolute phenol or pure carbolic acid, used in the proportion of 1-400th in the syrup fed to the bees.

Mr. Cheshire considers that the queen must not be removed; but on the contrary, if it is intended to save the combs, I have found the first step towards a rapid recovery is made by deposing the reigning queen, and giving a young and vigorous queen bred from clean stock, when the entire attitude of the bees is changed, and great determination and energy takes the place of the former utter inability to clear out the foul stuff.

If the disease begins in early spring it is very likely the colony will go down hill at a rapid rate, while the remnant will not be worth troubling with, and should be cleared out by fire after sulphuring the bees. This should be done in the evening when all the other stocks are quiet, taking care to foul as few things as possible ; burn all you use that is not of much value, and the rest disinfect thoroughly with a solution of carbolic acid, 1-200th part in water. If hives can be first steamed or scalded it will be a great advantage.

## Rational and Simple Cures

for foul brood have been so long known to many practical bee-keepers, that it seems strange there are others quite unable to cope with the disease when it makes its appearance in their apiaries. The cause of this in the first instance must be inex-perience, but on the other hand where the inability to cure can not be put down to wilful negligence it is almost certainly through want of *caution*. The disease has been cured in the past, and can as readily be cured to-day. There is really no excuse whatever for the continued existence of foul brood in any apiary, in the light of facts already placed before bee-keepers.

Cures have been effected, in some instances apparently, by the aid of some one or other of the many much-vaunted remedies to be carried out without removal or destruction of the diseased combs ; but the continued advocation of these plausible cures, for general application, is nothing but a snare and delusion, and the greatest hindrance of any to the entire eradication of the disease.

## My own Experience*

occurred some twelve years since, and a cure was effected by removing the bees from their combs, and confining them in a.

---

* " A Practical Experience with Foul Brood, and How Cured." 3d., of
J. Huckle, King's Langley, Herts.

box or skep until a few began to drop exhausted from the cluster. They were then returned on to frames with starters or foundation, and having consumed all the diseased honey while in confinement, the complaint did not again appear. Though sometimes recommended, the honey is not worth the risk of feeding back to the bees after boiling; then there is the extractor contaminated, and a hundred other chances of extending the operations of the disease by a little carelessness or want of thought by the inexperienced.

Both Mr. Cowan and Mr. Cheshire appear to consider that honey does not contain the germs of disease; but that it does, and is the most fatal means of communicating foul brood, I have had opportunities of proving to my own cost.

Everything used when manipulating a diseased stock, including the hands, must be thoroughly disinfected before another hive is opened, and in every way the bee-keeper should be on his guard;

## "CAUTION!"

must be his watchword, and extreme vigilance will bring its early reward.

### Another Plan of Immediate Renovation

of my own is carried out by placing diseased bees immediately upon a new set of combs, the whole of which have just previously been filled with phenolated syrup by the aid of a large syringe, as explained later under "Feeding." The novice will do better to destroy every vestige of the original combs at once, together with the frames and hive, if not of much value; but the more experienced bee-keeper might think it worth while to save them. In that case *every* capped cell of food and brood must be raked open, and those combs in like manner be filled with phenolated syrup, immediately after being cleared of the bees. These combs may then be returned

F

are very badly smeared they should be removed and clean substituted.

Dysentery is very readily induced by any exciting cause, after the bees have been a long time without a cleansing flight. Thus, a stock, apparently in the best possible condition, may from some quite avoidable occurrence have its entrance choked by dead bees, and then the more prosperous the colony, the more disastrous will be the result.

By far the greater number of cases may be put down as being directly caused by starvation. A small lot of bees unable to reach stores situated away from the cluster, will generally perish without excitement during a too-long spell of cold, the cluster remaining unbroken just as the bees rested upon the combs. But take the case of a strong stock, particularly where a patch or two of brood has been started, and instead of continued cold compelling them to remain and die where they sit upon the combs, their very strength is the cause of their own destruction. They generate too much heat to remain quietly clustering where all the store within reach is at last exhausted. Though too cold yet for individuals to reach the more distant, but still plenteous store, the bees fully aware of their critical position, soon arrive at an excited condition, the temperature goes up rapidly, the cluster expands, and the lately unapproachable stores are within reach. But the instinct of self-preservation does not allow them to count the cost—the tremendous discount thus made upon their vital energies; neither can they avoid the fouling of their once clean, sweet smelling home.

Should a warm day soon follow this untoward excitement, the after effects are to a certain extent modified, as a good cleansing flight can be taken; but when the cold still continues, the bees never again being able to regain their former state of semi-hibernation, drag out their existence wandering aimlessly about, and die at a rapid rate, each day adding to the accumulated filth of the hive.

## Prevention.

This form of starvation, with its possible consequences, is to be avoided by seeing that every hive has heavily stored combs of good sealed food to winter on. A stock fed with ten or twelve pounds of thick warm syrup, rapidly, towards the end of September will store such food in the immediate vicinity of the cluster, and will stand well, until the following Spring is warm enough for the bees to move freely about the hive. Dysentery will probably never follow after such a provision has been made, unless through carelessness some other exciting cause, such as a choked entrance, badly fitting roof, &c., is permitted.

## Another Item

of considerable importance as a preventive, is the adoption of a large frame, when a greater store of food will always be found within reach of a more compact cluster. In a semi-hibernating condition, during cold weather a cluster of bees has no difficulty in gradually moving along the surface of the same combs, and can do so without there being any reason for excitement, but when it becomes necessary to shift on to an entirely fresh set, it means, as we have already seen, a disastrous disturbance of their natural economy.

CHAPTER IX.

# MODERN HIVES.

## HOW CONSTRUCTED AND FURNISHED.

THE chief feature of the Modern hive is that each comb
is built in a separate frame, enabling such to be removed at will without force, and without in any way soiling
or injuring the comb.   Each frame stands about ⅜-inch from
its neighbour, and 1½-inch from the centre of one to that of
the next, though this space may be varied to suit different
requirements as hereafter shewn.   The frame rests only upon
or in the hive proper by a lug or ear at each end, and a space
of not more than ⅜-inch must be allowed between the two end
bars of the frame and the walls of the hive; while not less
than ½-inch should be provided between the bottom rail and
the floor; or ¼-inch at the sides.

I present to the reader a simple hive with frames of the
Standard size as used generally at the present time; and
another hive with the same frames, equally as simple, but more
complete, having an outer case.   Also a very practically arranged hive with frames 16-inch by 10-inch, the more suitable
size for commercial, as indeed for all highly profitable purposes.

Fig. 5.

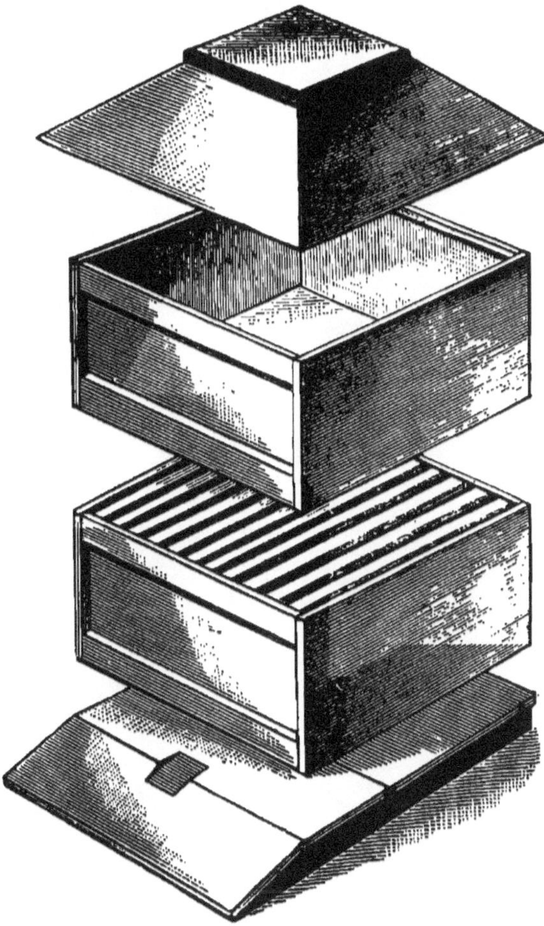

Fig. 8.
Design of " Economic Hive."

Fig. 6.
Position of Frame
resting on zinc runners.

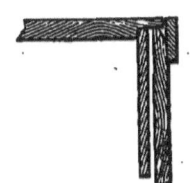

Fig. 7.
Frame end resting
on bevelled edge.

## THE ECONOMIC HIVE.

·This is a most simple and yet substantial hive, made from
¾-inch white deal. It contains nine frames and two dummies,
and the width of the hive inside, measuring across the frame,
is 16 inches. By removing the dummies there is room for
eleven frames for ordinary spacing, or as designed for close
spacing in the first instance, twelve may be used only ¼-inch
apart. I have practised crowding and close spacing ever
since foundation first came into use, finding it gave a more
compact brood nest and less room for stores below.

The same idea has since been brought forward in America,
with the claim that it prevented the issue of swarms, as the
bees would not, it was supposed, store in such shallow cells as
this arrangement enforced, and on the other hand would be
prevented from breeding in the thicker store combs (sections)
above. In neither case, however, is this correct, as I have
many times noted that not only do bees store and cap combs
which are even thinner than required for brood, but also that
the thickness of the combs in sections above is not the least
hindrance to the bees breeding there, as they simply reduce
the length of the cells to suit their purpose should the queen
be crowded by mismanagement below.

The Economic has a floor composed of one piece of board
17¼ inches by 11 inches, and another 5¼ inches wide of the
same length. The two are halved together, and a ¼-inch
rabbet cut out round the upper edge to keep wet from settling
under. Another 5¼-inch board, bevelled on the edge, forms
the flight board, and is detachable, being secured by simple
hooks, or hinged, if desired; the object being to ensure
that there is no projection in the way when packing and
travelling.

The front and back boards are each 16 inches long by 8⅝
inches deep. Both of these are bevelled along the upper edge,
to give a thin ledge for the frames to rest upon. The two side
walls are each 17¼ inches long by 9 inches wide, and overlap

the back and front walls so far that exactly 14½ inches are allowed between the two, being ¼-inch to spare beyond the length of the 14-inch standard frame at each end. A plinth, 16 inches by 2½ inches, is inserted at the top and bottom between the two 9-inch sides, filling in the space left at the ends of the top bars, and at the same time being a very convenient arrangement for lifting the hive. The permanent entrance is three inches wide and cut out of the floor, but full width can be given by sliding the hive forward.

## The Cover

is cut from 11-inch stuff as shewn in Fig. 9; the long edge being 21 inches and the other 7½ inches. The bevelled edges for mitreing at the joints are cut off on the saw bench, but where such cannot be obtained, the inside edge should be gauged at ⅜-inch, and then planed down to the mark, leaving the outside edge untouched. Nail together with at least five 2-inch brads down each side. The top square is nine inches across and screwed on from inside. There is no economy in planing the wood other than on the outside; but where this is not done it requires very much more paint, and is liable to rot, as the surface cannot be so well covered.

The Standard frame and dummy are as represented, Figs. 10 and 11; the top bar of the former being ¾-inch thick instead of the usual weak bar of only ⅜- inch thickness. The top bar may be either ⅞-inch or 1-inch wide.

All covers must be painted also on the lower edge and two or three inches up underneath as well. The floor requires painting at least three inches from the edge all round both top and bottom, as also the bottom edges of all compartments. This is too frequently omitted, when the hive does not last a fourth of the time it should. So long as all in sight is painted that is generally considered sufficient, whereas the very parts left undone happen to be the most vital, as it is at the joints that the wet settles and soon causes mischief.

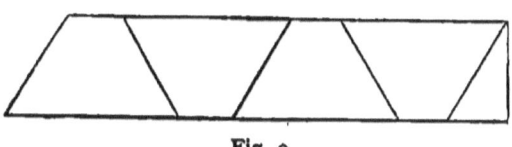

Fig. 9.

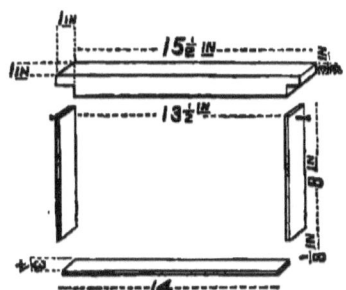

Fig. 10.
Standard Frame.

Fig. 11.
The Feeding Dummy.

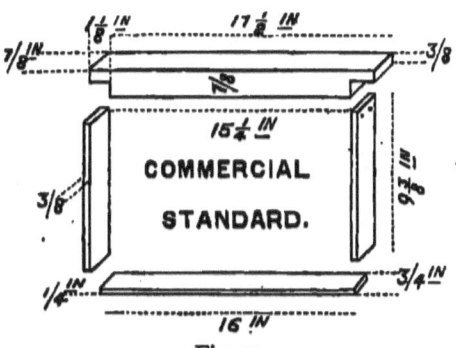

Fig. 12.

## THE CONQUEROR HIVE.

In hive construction I now present the very novel feature of whole bodies HANGING as do the brood frames, and notwithstanding the clear bee-space allowed all round between each upper and lower rim of the respective boxes, the sections are carefully secured against cold by the judicious arrangement of the quilting; while upward ventilation, around the sides may be allowed or entirely prevented at will, simply by the careful adjustment of the same.

This hive, which I have had under serious consideration ever since my Non-Swarming System was inaugurated, is in many important particulars quite different to any yet introduced; but there were several points which needed careful attention before I could carry out some desired improvements, and yet secure all, and more than all, the advantages claimed for excluder zinc, without using that expensive article unless in preventing the exit of drones.

My Non-Swarming Plan has been before beekeepers for some years, and has met with approval from all who have followed the plan intelligently; but so many of the hives in use are unsuitable for carrying out the method, that the novice has often found it difficult to adopt with the hives he has on hand. I therefore introduced during the season 1889-90 the above improved Non-Swarming Hive, which gives, (1) plenty of room in the right direction, (2) perfect ventilation at all seasons of the year without draught, (3) the most complete shade during the hottest days of summer, (4) the greatest ease in manipulation, as the lower body may be examined, also the upper, or brood nest proper, QUITE INDEPENDENTLY OF EACH OTHER, also without removing the supers. The latter points in particular, will be welcomed by many bee-keepers, who, while anxious to examine the brood nest or non-swarming chamber under it, frequently neglect to do so rather than be obliged to shift the whole lot. For a period extending over a term of fifteen years I have had hives in use having a deep outer case, and from these my best results have almost invariably been secured.

Inside, we have first the lower chamber (whether shallow or full depth, arranged for prevention of swarming) which touches neither the floor nor stock chamber above it, thus entirely doing away with propolisation at these points, and enabling such non-swarming arrangement to be examined with ease at any time required. The brood chamber comes next, and on this the supers may rest if desired. The hive can also be used with neither of the boxes touching its neighbour ; or with the old-style close-fitting arrangements as may be required.

Room is allowed for three sets of sections where one is placed under the stock in place of another body of full size ; otherwise, two only, as it is not desirable to have a deeper case. The hive proper is capable of holding either eleven or twelve frames, while the lower chamber will take as many more. For extracting, another takes the place of the sections, so that in all, nearly three dozen standard frames may be used for that purpose.

The side walls of the body boxes are only $8\frac{1}{2}$-in. deep, yet the space between the respective chambers is so carefully regulated that the distance between the several tiers of frames never varies. There are no two level surfaces drop upon each other anywhere about the body boxes or supers, and therefore very little propolisation, and less risk of crushing bees.

Notwithstanding the open space between the lower and upper chamber (and the other compartments when so arranged), and around the same, it may be as well to meet any enquiry regarding this arrangement by at once stating that with empty frames having simple wax guides directly under the brood-nest, comb building will never be carried on outside of the hive proper, and seldom to any extent in the lower frames, where the surplus is properly looked after.

Fig. 13.
The " Conqueror " shewn with cover
and back removed.

## A COMMERCIAL STANDARD.

I-must state at once that the Standard frame of the British Beekeepers' Association is much too small for any bee-keeper who is attempting to produce honey on a wholesale scale. It is true I have been using the Standard frame largely for some years past, and expect to continue to do so as long as I supply bees to those who have adopted that size; but its use has only the more forcibly brought to my mind the decidedly superior advantages enjoyed when using a frame measuring 16 inches by 10 inches. Reference to the pages of the *British Bee Journal* will show that there were not a few who held out for a brood or stock frame of the above dimensions at the time the Association decided on the miserably small stock frame now almost universally used in this country, and conspicuous among the opposition was that veteran bee-master, Mr. C. N. Abbott.

It would indeed appear that almost the sole reason why the present Standard was adopted, was because of its near approach to that of the 'Woodbury' pattern, a slight alteration being made that it might accommodate six American 4¼-in. by 4¼-in. sections, and yet. in practice scarcely one bee-keeper in fifty has ever brought the stock frame into use for that purpose. This very doubtful advantage was probably the *only* reason, not that the majority prevailed, but why that majority existed at all, for it is certain there were few, if any, extensive honey producers present at the Association meeting which then decided upon establishing one of the most serious hindrances progressive bee-culture has had to contend with during the past decade.

Evidence in favour of the larger size, as giving greater security in winter; a larger population more rapidly developed in spring; less inclination to swarm; and at all times a more prosperous and profitable colony, with comparatively little trouble in maintaining that prosperity—has been accumulating right along, as shewn by the practical results secured from

G

such colonies as remained in the old frames used by myself and other apiarists, and which should have been, and will yet be recognised as the Standard frame of this country, viz. :— 16-in. by 10-in.

It does not denote progress to hold to a certain size of frame simply because that has once been stamped as the Standard of the British Beekeepers' Association, whose committee, because of its peculiarly exclusive organisation, was not in a position to deal 'understandingly' with the commercial interests of either the producing or manufacturing industry.

There has long been a smothered feeling of opposition in some quarters against the frame now in use, and yet there are many who refrain from raising a dissenting voice for fear of coming in contact with a recognized institution which has not one valuable point as a recommendation, nor a single excuse for its continued existence, seeing that every honey producer using the small frame is at a serious yearly loss, as he may soon ascertain on trial.

I have already endeavoured to induce beekeepers to adopt a larger frame in connection with hives in present use, but the greater depth was not in accordance with the general methods adopted for working surplus receptacles.   Such an objection does not exist in relation with the large frame formerly used, and the same supering apparatus may be worked on either the Standard or the 16in. by 10in. frames.

I have no wish to create confusion, or to induce loss by urging all to at once take up with the frame our old friend Abbott and other veterans attempted to have recognised as the British Standard.   That frame has most certainly been *proved*, and I therefore recommend it with confidence as being far superior to the present Standard for the production of honey on a *commercial and profitable* scale.

The Commercial Hive is used with eight frames and two dummies, 1½-in. thick, either packed or used as dry feeders; or the sides may be permanently packed, the object being to keep as *narrow* a brood nest or cluster as possible, in oppo-

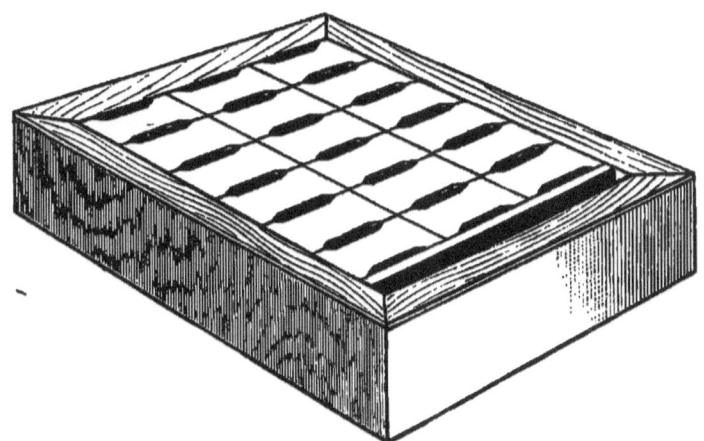

Fig. 14.
Commercial Super.

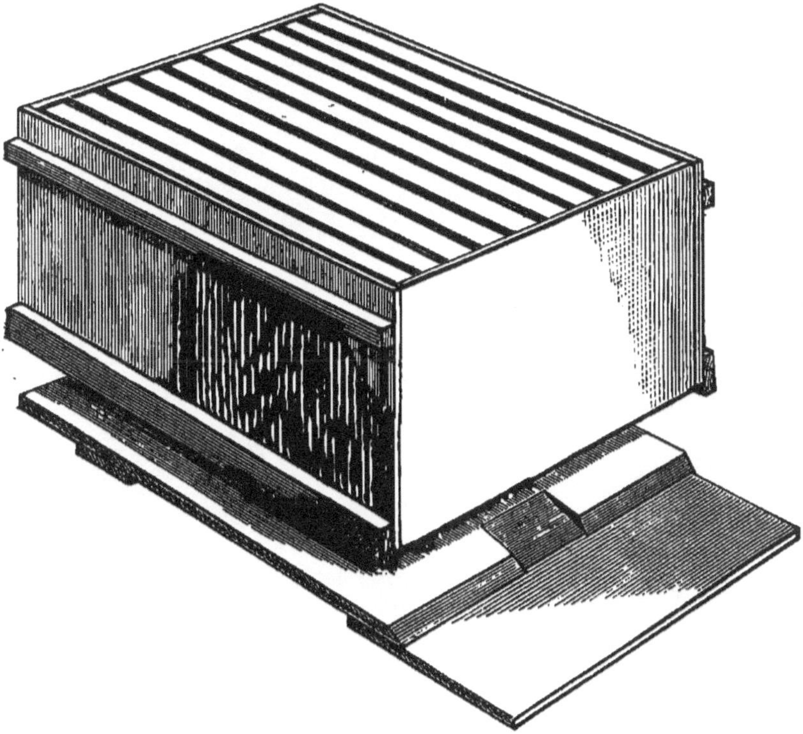

Fig. 14.
The Commercial Hive.

sition to the usual plan of adopting a wide supering surface above a shallow chamber. The latter does not give sufficient *power* below, neither does it properly economise power for the rapid and perfect production of section honey above it, as does a narrow but more populous cluster among our eight large frames, which arrangement provides for the more economic distribution and conservation of heat.

The principle of a *narrow deep cluster* must be continued throughout the whole tier of sections as well, and hence each crate of sections contains only three rows of six sections. I have tried varying numbers upon different surfaces and find it a serious error to attempt to crowd many sections upon an extended surface.

The section crates are double walled all round, and packed between, giving the most complete protection for the rapid perfecting of the combs of honey. The roof is made in the same manner as that illustrated for the Economic.

## SUPER CRATES

to hold from 21 to 27 sections, can be made as follows : Put together a plain box of the size desired with neither top nor bottom, and wide enough to take three 4¼-inch sections across besides the thickness of rails supporting them. Such rails are in the form of an inverted **T** ; the sections resting upon the ledges which must not be more than ¼-inch thick, giving that space between the sections and top bars of the frames. Any space left at the one end of the sections must be closed by a piece of wood to act as a dummy. This I prefer to fit only just tight, as both wedges and springs are quite unnecessary. With all crates in general use, the

### Space between the sections and top bars

of the frames is objectionable, in that brace combs are nearly always attached to the underside of the sections. To avoid this entirely, in 1881 I adopted a crate with the bottom composed of slats standing ⅜-inch apart.   When in position these slats come close upon the frames, but at *right angles* to them ; thus the bees have simply a number of small holes for passages —about ⅜-inch by ½-inch, which they are compelled to keep open ; no brace combs are built in consequence, as those are always continued from the wax that may be along the sides of the frame bars, when the old plan is allowed.   During the twelve years I have used this style of crate I have had no brace combs attached to my sections.

Fig. 16 will give a good idea of the manner in which the said square passages are formed ;  c being the bottom slats of the crate, and d the frame bars.

But now having the slats close upon the frames it will be readily understood that a full-sized crate could not be used without much inconvenience ; I therefore made it in two as seen in Fig. 17, each holding twelve to fifteen sections, and have had no more difficulty in removing one-half at a time than in taking out a frame of comb.   In replacing them a gentle horizontal motion will cause every bee to run down out of the way, though smoke first used will at once clear the course.

But perhaps the most important point with my twin crate, is that as the central combs are completed, by simply turning the outer row to the centre, the whole are finished off more evenly and in less time, and thus the usual outside thin sections are a thing of the past.

With this class of crate I have generally used my bee space sections giving their own passage under, but if the one-piece section is used strips ¼-inch thick should be inserted for the lower corners of the sections to rest upon.

## SECTIONS.

The one-piece sections wherein the new comb-honey is built are made in two forms, either with a bee space at top

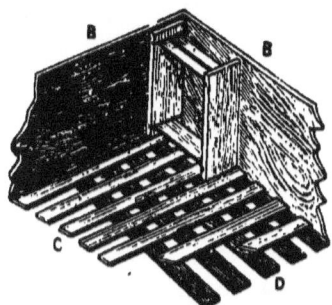

Fig. 16.
Position of Slatted Crate,
resting on Frames.

Fig. 17.
Twin Slatted Crate.

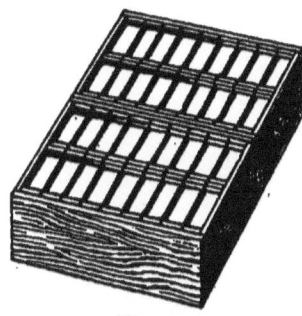

Fig. 19.
Simmins' Glass Rail Sections,
in Twin Crate.

Fig. 18.
Crate, with T Rests.

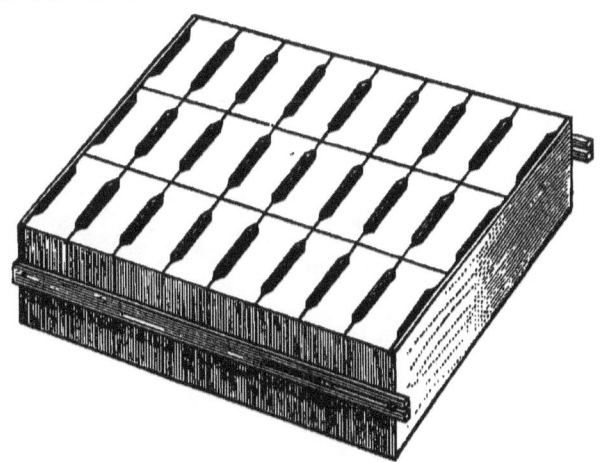

Fig. 20.
Simmins Simple Rack

and bottom, or such spaces on all sides. In the latter case it is proposed to give free communication throughout the entire crate instead of through each row of sections only. The advantages of intercommunication are doubtful, while the section of comb is certainly more difficult to handle, does not look so neat, and cannot be so conveniently packed for market as the old style.

The widths in general use are—2 inches to be used with separators, or 1¾ inches without; each 4¼ inches by 4¼ inches, to hold 1 lb. of honey. Sections to hold 2 lbs. are not in demand, but those to contain about one-half pound may generally be disposed of; these should be 1½ inches through, 4¼ inches deep, and barely 3 inches wide.

## Folding Sections.

By making a block to fit the inside of a section, fastening it horizontally to a table, the operation of folding can be carried through at a rapid rate, and one can always be certain of them coming true to square. With a lever and cramp motion to take the strain at two opposite corners, the tenons may be locked together as fast as the sections can be laid on the block. In dry weather these sections must first be damped at the V-cuts, or many will break.

The one-piece section has now taken such a hold in general estimation that no other style will ever supersede it; but where the apiarist has the time and convenience to make for his own use, my simple bee-space section will cost him even less than the other.

## Simmins' Bee-space Sections.

These were introduced some fourteen years since, and have been much appreciated wherever offered for sale. Glass was used for the top and bottom rails in the first instance, and the top rail was split to receive foundation.

The side bars are each 4¼-inches long by 1¾-inch wide, with a sawcut across each end, at ¼-inch from the edge, into which the top and bottom rails (1/16th inch thick), are fixed securely ; these being 1½-inch wide and 4⅛ inches (bare) long. For half-pounds the sides are 4¼ inches by 1½-inch, and the thin rails 1¼-inch by 2¾ inches.

If the sections are required flat, the top and bottom rails must be a little thicker, with a tongue and shoulder as shown by Fig. 27. In that case the sawcut in the side bars will be only the thickness of the horizontal rails from each edge.

## Separators

are made of either thin wood or tin, and are generally arranged to allow a space above or below them of not less than 3/16th inch from the upper and lower part of the sections. One with slots, suggested by "Amateur Expert," who contributes to the *British Bee Journal*, is illustrated (Fig. 28) with slots to correspond with the side bee-spaces in sections.

Where there are no side spaces in the sections, the slots are dispensed with.

## No Space between Supers.

Fig. 20 shows a still further development with regard to doing away with all intermediate spacing. This Rack is very simple, has no bottom rests at all, and allows the sections to stand close upon the frames and upon each other. Nothing can excel the simplicity and at the same time the efficiency of this arrangement. Practice absolutely confirms the fact that by dispensing with these useless passages, the surplus stored above the brood nest is largely augmented. In carrying, the sections are allowed to bear upon the side strip, and when not in use the racks lie flat and take up little room.

For years past I have persistently advocated the use of full sheets of foundation in sections, and found no better plan of securing such than by its insertion into my sections cut through on three sides, until in 1888 I designed my latest improvement in the shape of

## Completely Divided Sections.

The advantages of these are—(1) the foundation requires no -cutting up to fit into each separate section, (2) a full sheet of foundation, filling three sections at once, can be put in as quickly and much more securely than inserting a separate piece in a single section, (3) the foundation can first be worked out into comb, and without trimming or fitting, or cutting in any way, the same may be inserted immediately and securely into the respective sets. of three sections without any special fastening, (4) each set of three sections when in use and filled with comb can be handled in place of single sections, with no possibility of either falling out during manipulation.

My three-side-cut sections can also be used in the divided section frames, and answer equally as well when worked-out comb is not to be secured to start with, the sheet of foundation being placed across the three sections without cutting. This sheet of foundation is not quite the full depth of the frames, so that the usual stretching may be allowed for.

## CHAPTER X.

# COMB-FOUNDATION.

I HAVE been using this word while some of my readers may not as yet know what the article is. The two or three frames illustrated, showing the same in the centre, will convey some idea as to its use. This artificially made basis of new combs is really pure beeswax, and the sheet is first obtained by dipping nicely planed pine boards into the hot wax ; the plain sheet thus made is afterwards passed between rollers, which are so engraved as to give the wax the exact form and appearance of the natural mid-rib of all comb as the bees make it when left to their own devices, except that the comb foundation made by man gives the base of a more perfect, because more regular, comb than the insects themselves produce. The foundation is gauged to the size of worker cells (five to the inch); therefore, drone cells, and consequently drones, are excluded, while our combs are as flat as boards.

According to the thickness of the sheet required, whether for thin super foundation or for use in the stock frames, so many dips have to be made before the wax is peeled from the boards. Of these, two or three sets are required on hand standing in water, to give time for cooling and saturation.

There are a number of machines in use such as the Pelham, Root, Dunham, Given, Van Deusen, &c. Of these, the latter gives the most beautifully finished foundation I have seen, but, being flat bottomed, the bees appear to waste much time in converting to the natural base; though it must be acknowledged that in doing so comb is produced that has so thin a septum as to be equal to any all-natural comb. I have been very favourably impressed with the Pelham foundation, principally because there is no pressure on the side walls; but I suppose this might be so with all machines if thinner sheets were used, so that the same need not receive sufficient pressure to be driven tight into the matrice, while the same thin base would be retained. There is no advantage in having high side walls in super foundation, as I find the same nearly always scraped off to the base before actual building is commenced by the bees. Indeed, what I should consider a perfect super foundation would have nothing whatever but the bare base of the cells.

Foundation in the brood chamber gives a great saving in time under some conditions, as hereafter noted, but there are times when it is an unnecessary expense, more especially when the beekeeper has all the stock he requires, when he will become a producer of wax instead of a consumer of that article.

## How to insert Foundation in Frames and Sections.

The original method, and one practised by the late Mr. Raitt, myself, and others, is by melted wax run along the sheet of foundation on both sides where it meets the top bar. A board, 7 inches wide and 13 inches long, has screwed on the back two strips of ¾-inch stuff, which project about an inch over. The two projections on one side I have arranged as shown (Fig. 29) with a wide-headed screw to each, enabling the gauge to be regulated to a nicety. When set upon the inverted frame it stands ⅛-inch off from the centre of the bar, thus providing for the thickness of the foundation that it may hang exactly in the centre.

## Simmins' Divided Section and Holder.

The foundation is secured to one-half of this section frame, or holder, by using a flat blade which is rapidly pressed along the edge as it lies on the top bar, at intervals of about 1-inch. The ends are not to be secured. The foundation is either first worked into comb, or the halved sections immediately placed on either side. Three halves lying on a flat surface are first covered with the half-frame having the sheet of foundation, when the blank half with the other portions of the sections is put to them, the foundation lying between.

## For Melting Wax,

use a common glue pot, with a small brush to dip in, allowing the drip to run down the angle, joining the foundation and frame securely. Remove the gauge-board while reversing and then wax the other side, with the frame always held at a slight incline, starting the wax at one end, and allowing so much that it will just run to the other end. Be careful that the wax is kept at an even temperature, over a small paraffin stove; if too hot it will weaken the sheet, and if too cool it will not hold the foundation in place.

## Other Plans

are such as have the top bar split nearly its whole or entire length to receive the sheet of foundation, when two or three nails or screws are driven through, holding the two halves together with the impressed wax between. There is little economy in so weakening and disfiguring one's furniture permanently simply for this one preliminary operation, while the open cut along the top of the bar is the very best harbour for the wax moth, as the covering over the frames adds still further protection to such crevices.

＼ As a matter of fact, I have had no difficulty in getting combs built out perfectly true from foundation simply waxed

Fig. 21.
Three Side Cut Section. Introduced 1887.

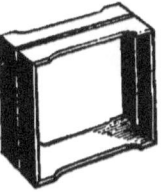

Fig. 22.
The same folded.

Fig. 23.
Simmins' Divided Section Holder,
shewing arrangement of foundation
and halved sections.

Fig. 24.
Completely Divided Section in the flat.

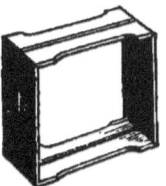

Fig. 25.
The same folded.
Introduced 1889.

to the top bars; but the frames *must* be placed closer together, so that many bees do not cluster upon any one sheet. Through many apiarists failing at this point, foundation for brood frames has been made much too heavy, being only four or five sheets (standard) to the pound; whereas I have no trouble in working full sheets at eight feet to the pound; indeed, ten feet to the pound have been frequently worked without sagging.

### Where Swarms are Hived upon Foundation,

the frames should be spaced not more than $\frac{1}{4}$-inch apart, with very light covering for the first few days, and a wide entrance.

Those who desire extra tough combs and well-filled frames, will find the most satisfactory plan to be that of

### Wiring the Frames.

This is done by piercing holes through the top and bottom of the frames about two inches apart to receive the wires, while another is run from side to side in the shape of the letter V. I prefer the parallel wires to run from side to side (Fig. 30) as the bottom rail is generally too weak to stand the strain, but in this case the sheet of wax must be secured to the top bar. Fine tinned wire is used for the purpose, and the starting point and finish should be at the same place where both ends are wound round a tack, which is then driven home, holding all securely. See that all the wires are drawn tight; place the sheet of foundation on your block; the wired frame upon that, and now press the wires into the mid-rib. Various instruments are used for the purpose, but a

### Simple Imbedder

can be made from a common nail filed up round at the point, with a slight indentation to run over the wire, which can be used at a rapid rate with a convenient handle. If the instru-

H

ment is used cold the point must be frequently passed over a cloth saturated with oil.

Mr. A. I. Root, editor of *Gleanings*, and others in America, have been quite successful in the use of an electrical battery on a simple scale, and they find the process of imbedding the wires thereby far more rapid and satisfactory than hitherto.

## Sections should be Filled

with new white combs if possible, and never with anything less than full sheets of foundation.   The former should be cut to go in tight ; the latter, when used in sections having no saw cuts, with about $\frac{1}{8}$-inch to spare on two sides, and fastened by melted wax at the top.   For gauging to the centre, use a block similar to that for large frames, but regulating screws can be placed on each of the four projections, so that the same block will do for any width of section.

Another plan is to make a saw-cut in the one-piece section as already shewn, and when folded the foundation is readily inserted in such a manner that the most perfect combs are obtained, while for packing to travel long journeys, both this and the completely divided section give greater security than is obtained by any other plan.

CHAPTER XI.

# HOW TO STOCK THE FRAME HIVE.

I HAVE shown the reader how to construct and furnish his hive, and will now explain the different methods employed for stocking the same.

The most simple way is to insert a swarm. Good swarms of native bees can generally be bought from a cottager in May for 10s. or 12s. each. They would, in that case, be brought home in a skep towards evening, when they may be shot out upon the frames spaced as already shown and provided with foundation, when a piece of ticking should be laid over them so as to not quite cover the whole surface of the hive, when all will soon draw below. When they are quiet, arrange the quilt carefully and place on the cover, and give an entrance at least six inches wide. As the centre combs are built out and filled with eggs, part them and insert one or two of the outside frames of foundation in the centre of the cluster until eight or nine are well filled. By this time close the entrance to about 1½-inch, having previously added warmer material above, such as two or three thicknesses of carpet above the ticking or a tray of chaff or cork dust two inches thick.

### Best Time to Transfer.

Where one has straw skeps he will desire to transfer his bees to the frame hive. This can be done in April to great advantage, as it is just then that the stimulation does most good, and excites the bees to extend the brood nest.

The bees are first to be removed from the skep by either of the methods before mentioned (Chap. II.), when the best combs are to be cut to the right size to fit exactly tight into the bar-frame ; all edges being cut quite square so that they go together well, and can be more readily secured by the bees. Tie two or three pieces of ¼-inch tape round the frames to keep all in place, and return the combs to the bees, which may first be shot into the bar-frame hive. They will soon draw among the newly-transferred combs and clean up their house, where, after a day or two, one will hardly tell where the joints were. Close up with division boards, cover up warm, and keep the entrance not more than one inch wide until it is absolutely necessary to make it larger. The patches of brood must be arranged so that the larger are at the centre, and the smaller graduating to either side, thus securing greater protection. Should the bees appear crowded with only the combs transferred, give a frame of foundation in the centre, and another as soon as they begin to cluster on the outside of the division board. Feed carefully so that there is always a little store in hand, but not enough to hinder the operations of the queen. Continue such stimulation until honey comes in.

It is so frequently recommended that the contents of fixed-comb hives should be transferred twenty-one days after swarming, that I consider it advisable to show that this waste of time is quite unnecessary. The swarm should be hived upon six or seven sheets of foundation close to the parent colony and facing the same way. Within ten days the young queens will be hatching out when a cast or second swarm would issue from the old stock. This appears to have been overlooked ; therefore I advise transfering on the seventh day after the issue of the first swarm, first carefully removing one of the queen cells before druming on the hive. While shifting the combs, cut out all the other royal cells, and after the operation return the one previously removed, which meanwhile should have been placed above the first swarm between the quilting to prevent chill. As soon as the young queen hatched therefrom is laying freely, destroy the other and unite the two colonies on the second evening following, when supers may be at once put on.

It is better that transfering operations be carried out in some warm room, or manipulating house, first laying a sheet of paper on the table whereon the tapes are to be arranged, with the frames on those, so that all is in readiness for tying as soon as the combs are fitted. While it is not absolutely necessary that the combs be fitted in just the same way up as they were built, it is not desirable to have them inverted, but to save material it is often advisable to put them in on end, or half inverted, as I have done for many years past. Certainly there is the brood to handle if transferred before the twenty-one days have expired, but with ordinary care this is not damaged, except where the knife cuts a straight line, and that is far preferable to having the combs full of honey.

## Other Plans of Transferring,

such as the following, may commend themselves to either the novice, or those who have little time to spare.

The first is to place the fixed comb-hive upon the frames of the modern hive, with a slatted board between, and allow the bees to work downwards on the combs or foundation placed for them. Towards the end of the season the stock will have its brood located in the frames, while honey will probably occupy the whole of the upper combs. This can then be removed, but the stock must not be allowed to starve, as it is quite likely very little store will be in the brood combs.

The other method is that of placing the skep or other fixed comb-hive in an inverted position immediately *under* the frame-hive, allowing communication through an opening in an improvised floor. In this case the inverted combs will be gradually emptied of everything. The stock will then take up its abode in the frames, and also work in supers above. These empty combs can then be transferred at leisure.

CHAPTER XII.

# GENERAL MANAGEMENT.

WHILE it is my intention to go through twelve months'
management, and as everything depends upon proper
treatment at this period, I shall begin with the

## AUTUMN.

If the apiarist keeps only young queens he will have not
need to stimulate the hive for the production of young bees at
this time; while the *only reliable stimulation* for early spring
breeding is secured by correct autumn preparation.   If any
colony has not sufficient food to last till the following April,
give all it wants rapidly before the end of September.   Among
novices there is much uncertainty as to the quantity required
to store a colony for winter, but not less than six square feet
of sealed comb (including both sides) should be provided; if
more, so much the better:  but on no account should weak
stocks, if allowed to stand, be forced to store beyond their
actual capabilities.   Thus if in August a stock covers only
six combs, there are not sufficient workers to store more
than one-half that number of combs, and that quantity will
certainly be enough and to spare for their needs.  (See Feeders
and Feeding.)

### Unite Stocks of doubtful Strength.

As mentioned elsewhere, all weak colonies must be united
before feeding takes place; and not simply weak lots, but others

about which there is the slightest doubt as to them coming through all right. The reader will ask: "How are those others constituted about which there can be any doubt, other than really weak stocks?" In the first place I should say those which have old, or otherwise unsatisfactory queens; those which through any oversight may have been without a laying queen for a few weeks during the latter part of the summer; as well as those which may be short of stores. It will be found impossible to alternate the combs with ten or eleven-frame hives where they are populous, and in that case place the whole hive upon another near to it; or if a little too far apart, bring each hive half-way; and in all cases of uniting, place a wide board from the ground to the flight board, not only to attract the flying bees, but also that both lots may be aware of a strange location, and so have no inclination to fight. (Refer to Uniting.)

## What is a Strong Stock?

Will be a frequent question. Can I explain the situation fully? I will endeavor to do so for the benefit of the many who never seem to realise that ' Unity is strength,' and that nothing less than the most intense power, as exhibited in the almost hurricane strength of profitable colonies, will ever bring them a reliable income year after year.

You want for the production of honey just that strength of numbers which turns the ordinarily gentle workers into ever suspicious defenders of their home, ready to assail, if need be, any intruder who disturbs them without due precautions! You want during the summer that teeming hive which all day long shows you such a continuous stream going and coming, that the tiny insects appear almost thicker than hailstones! You want, after the removal of the surplus receptacles, a hive of ten or twelve frames so over-crowded that great lumps of clustering bees hang outside until really cold nights compel them to crowd inside!

Do you want honey ?   Honey by the hundredweight and by the ton ?   Then again read, and re-read the commencement of this chapter, and let the autumn not pass without a general renovation and uniting of poor colonies.   Pray do not. cling to those miserable weaklings, fearing you are sacrificing all hope of future *increase*.   Ah ! that is just the word ; in the completion of that last sentence is found the whole trouble. How many there are who cannot bring themselves to ' close down ' their scattered forces, and so make their chances of wintering almost certain, and positively securing stocks which will give six times the increase (if required) that any three weakly lots would do, even supposing the latter will all winter safely.

So far as food and strength are concerned, we are now ready for

## WINTER,

and the next thing to be considered is whether or not more warmth, in the shape of packing, is required.   Mr. Raitt said that the best packing for bees in winter is " bees," and I quite agree with him ; in fact I use nothing more about my hives than they have had all the summer, and at all times consider that the most vital point is the top of the hive, where they are always covered with warm material, such as chaff, or cork-packed trays, pieces of carpet, or sacking.

It is not important whether there are chaff-packed dummies on the outsides of the brood nest, or not ; though of the two I give the preference to old tough combs.

### Position of Frames.

All hives should stand so that the frames are "end on " to the south wall, that every seam of bees is warmed up during each gleam of winter sunshine, enabling them to change their position and take food, while bringing stores nearer the cluster. Bees will winter all right if so situated and in good heart, but where placed behind thick walls, they are subject to a continued low temperature, as the mid-winter sun does not penetrate to the cluster. There is no warmth in double walls at this time, just when it is most required, though of course I admit that they are a benefit as soon as the cluster expands, retaining the heat given out by the bees; but this does not compensate for the greater disadvantage in mid-winter as before mentioned.

Mr. Abbott, when editor of the *British Bee Journal*, was quite aware of the immense advantage of admitting the sun's rays during winter, and recommended that a piece of glass be let into the outer wall of double-sided hives. However, double-packed walls to hives do not pay for the extra expense as compared with single walls, and besides being more cumbersome, are a positive nuisance during the heat of summer, when shade only is required, rather than additional heat. For as a matter of fact packed walls cannot be cool in summer, as the advocates of the same would have us believe. Why the more frequent swarming complained of with these? and are we not told that more warmth is given in winter? how much more then, *in excess*, in summer?

One thing of the utmost importance to which I have often had occasion to call attention, is the

## Space below the Frames.

The regulation distance of ⅜-inch is certainly allowed between the bottom rail of the frame and the floor of the hive when first made, but this is not enough, as the exposure causes the side walls to shrink fully one-fourth of an inch. This makes it quite inconvenient and disagreeable in replacing frames, as well as where hives are tiered up; and though ⅜-inch clear may not work quite well between upper stories at first, it will soon come right by shrinkage when anything like 9-inch stuff is used, though it may be considered that the wood has been already well seasoned. Now the ⅜-inch space is not sufficient for winter, and where a lower rim cannot be added to the hive, a circular hole should be cut in the centre of the floor board, about 2 inches in diameter, which will greatly assist ventilation, while providing the inmates with a ready means for disposing of their refuse, dead bees, &c.　Failing either of the foregoing, the frames can be raised by placing ¾-inch strips under the projecting ears.

Dysentery and other ills are brought on by the too common neglect of this matter, dead bees drop to the floor and clog the too shallow space under the frames, then getting into a mass ventilation is impeded, and when a fine day does occur the bees have enough to do to find the entrance, while the dead and rubbish remain untouched, only to be added to during the next cold spell.　Insufficient ventilation and foul matter now begin to tell upon the constitution of the population, and there is little chance that the stock will ever be of much use unless it has immediate attention, as many of the bees are now unable to fly when warm days do offer them a chance ; particularly is this the case where the frames run across the entrance with double walls.　With single walls and the frames end on to the entrance the bees are not so liable to be blocked in.

## Covering above Frames.

Much uncertainty exists among novices as to whether the frames should be covered with porous or non-porous material ; but, dear Reader, it is just this : if you use porous material above your winter cluster, an entrance not more than three inches in width should be allowed ; if a non-porous covering such as American oilcloth be used next above the frames (of course with warm material above that), then a wider entrance must be provided according to the strength of the colony.

## A perfect Winter Arrangement

of the combs is secured in the manner already shewn with reference to the description of the Conqueror hive.

A similar arrangement has long been used by myself with the Economic hive, by placing an empty chamber under the stock-hive, and this, though not so satisfactory as the other, is the best substitute.

With hives in general use I find the best way to secure ventilation to be as follows :—Place the combs to one end farthest from the entrance ; there may or may not be a dummy on that side nearest the vacant space, but such dummy must not touch the hive side, and will hang as an ordinary frame ; for my own use I prefer no dummy. Cover the frames with non-porous cloth as usual, but allow clear communication from the entrance to the roof, which is, of course, ventilated. Thus we have no draught *through* the brood nest, but a thorough ventilation in front of the same, with a certain change of air for the occupants of the hive.

As an instance, I have put up driven bees in Autumn on standard frames of empty combs ; closed up with chaff-packed dummies ; a medium entrance, and warm porous covering on top, with no through ventilation. They were fed carefully and had young queens. Others were made up on large frames (14 inches by 14 inches) of comb of the same strength, and the same food, but the combs were placed to one end of the hives where the wall was only ½-inch thick ; at the opposite side nothing protected the comb, while there was a large unoccupied space with three 2-inch holes in the side wall, and one in the centre of the floor. Communication was quite open to the roof, where there was ten times the space generally allowed for ventilating ; the frames were covered with porous material, and yet with all this extra ventilation and no dummies, these stocks came out 5 to 1 better than those prepared as usual on Standard frames.

Where bees are wintered on Standard frames in long hives, whether the brood nest is placed at the back or front of the hive, the dummy next the open space must stand *clear of the side walls,* just as the frame does. Those who have followed the advice sometimes given, to the effect that such dummy must be tight fitting and have an entrance of only two inches or less cut out of the bottom edge, will have reason to appreciate the loose fitting board.

When keeping bees in a loft, Mr. Cowan, the present editor of the *British Bee Journal*, raised the crown board of his hives with small pieces of wood, such as match ends, as well as giving the same space between the floor and body of the hive. Perfect ventilation was in this manner secured without draught, being in a large closed space; but the same plan could not be thought of with hives standing in the open.

Really there is nothing to be done to the bees during the winter months, and all the foregoing provisions have to be settled before the cold weather arrives. Cold, with judicious ventilation, and clear space under the frames, a good cover, plenty of stores, and stocks in good heart, can do no harm.

## SPRING.

About the 21st of December the queens will begin to deposit eggs; in due time the young will hatch out, and slowly the brood nest is enlarged, until by the time the older bees begin foraging, the consequent heavy losses are fully compensated by those brought to life while outside all appeared quiet.

The production of young bees at this early date is not always without intermission; cold in itself never hinders it, as the brood is at the very heart of the cluster, but if unable to obtain water for many days together brood-rearing ceases, only to be renewed as soon as the workers can get abroad. Pollen is as a rule always present in well-stored stock combs, and when this comes in freely (March to April), all fresh from the fields, the brood nest is rapidly extended. Now is the time to see that the bees have more than sufficient food to keep them going. With a good queen it can hardly happen that the combs will be too heavily charged with honey at this season, but by taking the outside combs, one at a time, and inserting them in, the centre of the brood nest after the cappings are first bruised, great progress will be made. One such comb as yet at an interval of seven or ten days, as needed, will keep the bees and queen busy, and by May 1st the whole ten or more combs will be one mass of brood, and the hive so crowded with bees that another set of combs will be required *below* the stock hive. If one has no combs on hand, then use sheets of foundation, alternating them with the combs of brood throughout both storeys, and see that the older brood goes below, with the pollen combs near the outside. Now proceed as explained for extracted honey, but if comb be desired let the lower storey have starters only in the frames. In any case feed from " hand to mouth," until honey comes in freely, as such a large population is liable to be rendered perfectly useless by the loss of the brood, by the slightest neglect at this time.

Where stocks cannot be got up to the desired strength for the opening of the

## SUMMER

season, or when one wishes to take every possible advantage of the harvest, he will not hesitate to work on

### The Doubling System.

At this moment honey may be coming in rapidly, with every appearance of fine weather to continue. The first is always the best chance, and it is a question whether the apiarist will simply allow the bees to waste their energies in excessive brood rearing, or at once cut short their work in that direction, and direct far greater power towards the " piling up " of stores. What is done must now be done quickly, and though the usual plan has been to simply place the brood combs of one stock with, or upon its neighbour, and saving the queen with the swarm thus made, the following definite methods of proceeding will give the highest profitable results.   For producing

## Comb Honey,

select any two desirable stocks standing near to each other. Unite the entire force of workers on to eleven frames of the most completely packed combs of brood; allow the non-swarming chamber under, and put on supers already filled with comb to the capacity of some 40lbs., or even more.   If the other queen is old, destroy her, otherwise reserve her majesty in a nucleus.   The surplus combs can be placed above any pair doubled for securing

## Extracted Honey.

In this case, after removing one queen, place one hive bodily upon the other, having first arranged the non-swarming chamber below all.   Thus· we have three chambers teeming with life, but at least one other must be added above with empty combs, or odd brood combs that may be left over from stocks united for surplus comb honey.   If foundation must be used in the absence of sufficient combs to fill further chambers, then it will be better to alternate frames of comb and foundation, to secure the more rapid completion of the latter.

Where extracted honey is to be largely worked for,

## Surplus Brood Combs

are the most valuable stock-in-trade the bee-keeper can have, if he only takes care when out of use to keep them in a dry store with free ventilation, and all vermin excluded.

## A Great Evil

noticeable in nearly all apiaries is the absence of any attempt to keep on hand a supply of surplus hives.   In calling attention to this, I have no intention whatever of seeking accommodation for swarms, but have in mind the best means of restraining them, and making far more profitable use of the ever swelling numbers in the mother hive.

What reasonable man can for a moment imagine he is to secure large results from the one brood chamber which still constitutes the rule in Modern (?) Bee-keeping? and this often with a fixed hinged cover as well as permanent legs, which the owner does not conceive the idea of removing!

A hive which does not permit of rapid extension either above or below the original brood chamber, by the seasonable addition of other like chambers always held in stock, is one more suitable for fire-wood than progressive bee-culture.

Further detailed management for the Summer season will be found fully explained in the following pages, where separate chapters will be devoted to the various necessary proceedings.

## CHAPTER XIII.

# SIMMINS' NON-SWARMING SYSTEM.

THIS System of Management was first made public by the issue of my Pamphlet on the subject in February, 1886. In the same work I claim that "*No colony in normal condition attempts to swarm unless it has all its brood combs completed*;" and, further: "To reduce the matter to a greater certainty, while admitting that bees may sometimes swarm if such open space and incomplete *brood* combs happen to be situated at the back, or the point farthest from the entrance, the author *insists that the open space and unfinished* STOCK *combs shall always be at the front, or adjoining the entrance.*" That is, at the front where long hives are used; or between (and under) the brood nest and the entrance where hives are tiered one above the other; the latter plan always being the more satisfactory for general working.

The idea had been long fixed in the minds of bee-keepers that unless the bees were crowded into the supers nothing would induce them to work there. On the contrary, however, I have had them storing freely in several sets of supers, while at the same time they had eleven empty " standard " frames immediately below the brood nest, with free communication between.

But an important item in the new management consists in supplying every section with fully-worked combs, so that the bees are induced to store above rather than build to any extent either in front or below, as the case may be, where frames with ¼-inch starters only are placed.

If through any inattention to the supers, or a sudden influx of honey, the bees have no room above, no time is lost, and they can go on building below. Nevertheless, these frames with starters must never be allowed to have finished combs, and should any be nearing completion they are to be cut out to be used in the sections, first extracting the honey if any, and exposing for two or three days those which may contain eggs, that they may be removed by the bees when such combs are returned.

## The Working of New Combs

is now more satisfactory, while the cutting of them up for sections can now be entirely avoided by the use of my completely divided sections and section holders.

When it is desired to draw out the foundation before placing the divided halves in position, a sheet is attached to one side of each *alternate* half of the section frames; or, in other words, only one-half of the sectional parts required, being furnished with foundation attached to the inner side, a shallow chamber is filled up with them, and placed next above the stock chamber as early as the bees can possibly be induced, by warmth and careful feeding, to work out the foundation rapidly. Any kind of hot water vessel placed above, especially at night, where it can be regularly attended to, will induce rapid work, so that three or four days only need elapse before the foundation is sufficiently worked out for removal.

The removed set may be placed above the quilt, and the section halves adjusted as soon as the bees go down, if not shaken off in the first instance. Another set may follow close on the brood nest, and when the season fairly opens these new combs will prove a remarkable stimulus, while the bees will then be strong enough to start other foundation in the lower chamber, used for the time being in place of, or next above, the swarm preventing chamber.

When the section halves are placed upon either side of the newly built combs, simple pressure under a board will fix all securely.

When combs are completed, remove the halved section holders and clear away all odd wax and propolis. Each set of three sections may be handled as one, or, if preferred, then divide with fine wire.

Let it be borne in mind that

## The True Principle of Management

*consists in so manipulating the supers that none of the frames with starters have finished combs* all the season.

The space below and in front of the brood nest gives ample ventilation, keeping the hive cool ; and the combs never being completed the desire for swarming does not exist.

As will be seen, the system is particularly applicable to the production of comb-honey, and without doubt is the only process that will prevent the issue of swarms while securing that article. At the same time it makes a greater certainty of prevention while working for extracted honey, though generally in getting the latter article stored no swarming will occur, as there is no object in having the combs well finished, and unlimited room can be given.

This is the first time the long-vexed question of prevention has been reduced to systematic management ; but, as usual with anything new, there are not wanting those who claim that there is nothing original in it. The editor of the *British Bee Journal* endeavoured to prove that it had been in use many years since, and that the Stewarton Hive was worked-upon the same principle ; and while attempting to shew how to produce comb-honey without swarming, I find he could not tell how to work *entirely* for that article with any given colony ; but only that a limited quantity could be obtained while at the same time using many combs under the sections as and for extracted honey—a most unsatisfactory process, by which few finished sections can be obtained unless my plan of filling the same with worked-out comb is adopted.

Bee-keepers generally have saved over unfinished combs in sections from year to year, and these were found to give a good start to the bees, but nothing was done to institute the systematic production of such new white combs for all sections before being placed on the hive until the present system was inaugurated.

All that has ever been given as to the manipulation of the Stewarton Hive relates chiefly to the insertion of several swarms into the set of boxes. This does not look like prevention, and moreover, whether with swarms or established stocks the principle did not consist in keeping the same or any empty chamber *always* below the brood nest. In hives 3 feet long it is claimed that in America the plan was tried 20 years since. The bees in this case working from back to front all on the same level. Here the combs were removed *as completed* at the front.

Just here the Reader will not fail to see the difference—a contrast decidedly in favour of my own plan, which is this : The surplus is worked and continually removed from *above*, while no attention is needed below or in front of the brood combs ; as in the first place no combs are there permitted to become completed, and the same frames remain in the same place all the season, because with careful attention above little or no comb is built in them, as my own experience has shewn.

While many consider that they have no need to prevent the issue of swarms, and can obtain better results by allowing one swarm to each colony, there are many districts where the season is of short duration, and the largest surplus is only obtained by prevention. The system, moreover, should be of advantage to all, enabling increase to be made at the most fitting opportunity ; and not, as is too often the case, just as a good honey-flow is on.

My non-swarming system is here illustrated for the better guidance of the Reader. Fig. 31 represents the manner of proceeding where long hives are used, with the empty frames arranged on the same floor, between the brood nest and entrance. Fig. 32 shews the plan adopted when tiering up, with the lower hive having empty frames. Both sectional views exhibit two crates of sections above the brood nest.

## The Worked-out Combs for Sections

are obtained by using foundation which runs nine or ten feet to the pound, having a very thin base, otherwise an objectionable mid-rib will be found in the centre of the combs.

All my other methods formerly used are giving place to that now adopted with my halved sections and section holders, which offer a perfect means of obtaining beautifully worked-out combs, which can be placed directly into the sections (or rather the halved sections placed upon that) without the trouble of fitting or cutting either them or the foundation in any way.

A sheet of foundation, about 13in. by 4in., is fastened on to the flat side of one of the half-frame section-holders. A number of these are worked out above a strong colony, which, if necessary, is carefully fed, and the foundation is soon ready to be placed over other stocks and they will not hesitate to complete the work so begun.

It is a mistake to suppose, as some do, that the foundation will in the first instance be drawn out to fully extended cells. Nothing but disappointment and loss of time would result with such an object in view. A day or two only should be allowed before the partly worked comb is removed and further sheets supplied for the same purpose.

The companion parts of the section holders as well as the halved sections are put together as already shewn under the chapter on ' Foundation.' Slight pressure secures all in place, when a most perfect arrangement is presented.

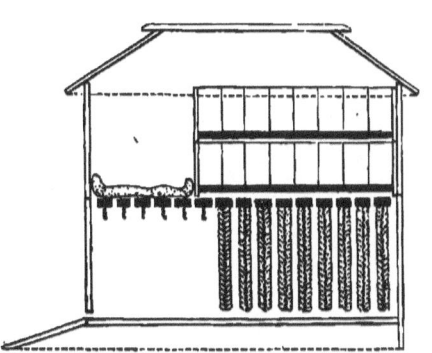

Fig. 31.
Non-swarming Plan, with Long Hives.

Fig. 32.
Non-swarming Plan,
with Tiering Hives.

Fig. 33.
Swarm Catcher.

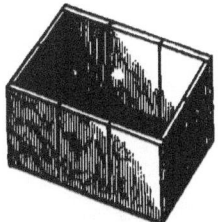

Fig. 34.
Comb Cutting Box.

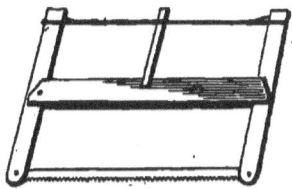

Fig. 35.
Comb Cutting Saw.

The gauged cutting box and the frame saw for cutting odd combs to fit into sections as hitherto used are shewn as Figs. 34 and 35. The blade of the saw is of the thinnest possible material, with very fine teeth.

## Swarm Attachments

for securing swarms when they issue, were devised by me in the year 1888, and for some years past similar contrivances have been mentioned both in English and foreign journals, though complete satisfaction seems seldom to have been attained by their use.

I still adhere to my non-swarming plan, or that which helps to restrain bees from the *desire* to swarm, as being by far the more simple and effectual, but as there are many who for various reasons are unable to control swarming, I illustrate my latest design in Swarm Catchers (Fig. 33), which requires little attention when once in position.

It is simply the arrangement of my usual swarm preventing chamber under the brood nest, with a floor between having a central opening covered with excluder zinc. The whole front of the lower chamber is covered with excluder zinc, set out 1½in., and reaching up to and covering the front of a porch which comes in front of the main entrance.

The alighting board has here several inverted cones so inserted that the queen failing to make her way out with the swarm finds a passage into the lower chamber from which she cannot return, and where the bulk of the swarm, after vainly seeking her abroad, re-assemble and go on to work. If allowed to continue there they work in connection with the original force; but, in this case, all surplus queen cells must be cut out, and the zinc removed from the upper entrance that the young queen remaining may leave for her natural purposes.

## CHAPTER XIV.

# THE PRODUCTION OF HONEY.

THE system hereafter to be described will be based upon the non-swarming principle just explained; the reader will therefore understand that though not always expressed, it is necessary that the vacant space, having only empty frames, be provided either below or in front of the brood nest, according to the style of hive in use.

## EXTRACTED HONEY

is that which is removed from the combs by centrifugal force, without breaking them up; while the liquid is consequently clear, and of far superior quality to that which by old-fashioned methods was obtained by straining the whole mass of honey, pollen, comb, and larvæ, through a cloth.

A common practice is to remove the honey before the cells are capped over, and large weights of such "green stuff" are often boasted of. As a matter of fact, however, such honey never equals that left in the upper tiers until thoroughly "ripened" by the heat and perfect ventilation of the hive. When the combs are at least two-thirds sealed extraction may commence, when generally an article of good consistency will be procured.

In the process of ripening, "green" honey loses considerable weight by evaporation of the excess of water, and being passed over a series of heated plates, its quality is inferior in every respect, as both the colour and usual characteristic aroma of honey is impaired. The sooner beekeepers give up these honey-ripening fads the better it will be for themselves and their customers ; the best article only is that which will create a demand.

The word "extracted " has been objected to in the *American Bee Journal* as being inappropriate, and that the consumer does not understand it. Nevertheless, the term will stand as long as the extractor endures ; and if the public mind is likely to be impressed with the idea that "extract of honey" is being offered, all the apiarist has to do is to show on his labels *why* it is called "Extracted" honey, and in what manner it is

PURE ENGLISH HONEY

*SUPPLIED DIRECT FROM*

The Southern Apiaries.

**N**ONE BUT PURE HONEY GRANULATES; when this has become so, it can be made liquid again (if desired) by placing the jar in another vessel containing hot water, when it will become as when first sealed up.

**NOTICE.**

**I** GUARANTEE this Honey to be quite pure, and free from the usual impurities of the old-fashioned "strained" honey.

This is "extracted" from the combs (without being broken in the least), by the aid of centrifugal force; hence its superior quality.

(Signed) **SAMUEL SIMMINS.**

removed from the combs ; as seen by a copy of my own label. The word "liquid" is certainly out of place, as our commodity is not always in that form, while the honey is liquid in our beautiful sections.

## Bottled Honey.

In glass the wholesale demand is generally for 1-lb. jars. The most popular kind is the jelly glass, and being in such demand the manufacturers are of course enabled to place them at a lower figure than any other kind. They are neat, elegant, and with a nice label, most attractive, costing 10s. 6d. per gross ; with corks, 12s. 6d.; so that including carriage, bottling, &c., the total cost is a little over 1d. each (Fig. 37). Half and quarter-pounds can also be retailed at home, but are useless to the trade.

The bottles illustrated are especially suited for honey. Fig. 36 makes a good exhibition bottle ; 37, the Greek design jelly glass ; 38, a bottle very much appreciated by customers generally. These are manufactured by " Breffits," 83, Upper Thames Street, London.

For bottling, the honey must be particularly clear; and whatever shade of colour it may have, it should be bright and in all cases as before stated of such a consistency that it " piles " up well when drawn off.

Fill all bottles as evenly as possible and cork up at once, driving the latter home with a mallet, while holding the bottle in the left hand clear of any bench or shelf. Having filled your bottles, of course those with corks need some finish, and for capping the whole nothing is more simple and inexpensive than

## Sealing Wax ;

but this article must be made at home. Procure common yellow resin and heat it above a small oil stove in an earthenware vessel, or if preferred a large glue pot. Use one part of beeswax to three of the other to toughen it and make it hold to the glass. Now an important item is the

## Colour

of the sealing wax. A *bright* colour will contrast well against the contents of the bottle, and the colouring matters used in common paint answer every purpose. Stir all thoroughly to get an even mixture, but at no time let the wax boil.

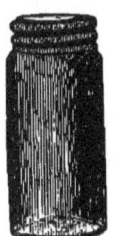

Fig. 36.

Fig. 37.

Fig. 38.

Fig. 39.

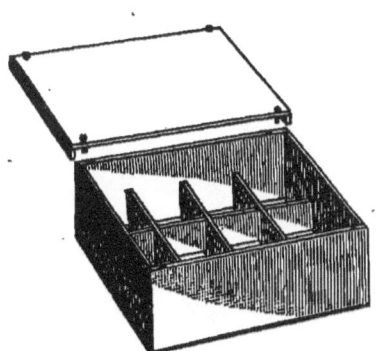

Fig. 40.
Bottle Crate for 1 doz.

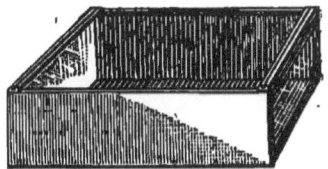

Fig. 41.
Comb Honey Crate.

## To Wax the Bottles

invert them with the cork and upper surface of the bottle just hidden in the heated substance for a moment. The operation can be rapidly carried out, and in lifting the bottles, give one or two turns that no bead of wax may run down the side. Now all is ready for the label, which must be of such a character as to contrast favourably with the contents.

## Canned Honey.

With prices much lower, together with a general and increasing demand, honey in tins is becoming popular. Two, three, and six pounds seem to be mostly in demand, and at reasonable rates large quantities of good honey can thus be disposed of. Colour is not of so much importance, and when granulated this is a good way to dispose of our produce ; but the article must be thoroughly ripened, and of good flavour. The most elaborate label that can be obtained is required to make tins attractive.

Bee-keepers frequently complain that they cannot dispose of their honey ; but if they only take the trouble to work their own neighbourhood at a *selling price* they will be surprised to find that instead of producing more than can be disposed of, they will be unable to supply the demand. Only recently I have been offered honey in considerable quantities at rates higher than what I could myself obtain ten years ago. Honey has to compete with many other articles, themselves much reduced in value in these "cheap times," and supply and demand must regulate the price.

- Having shewn how to prepare and market extracted honey, we have yet to consider the best means of obtaining it. First we must

## Provide for extracting

by arranging our hives in the best manner for its production. A good stock of worked-out combs is invaluable for this

purpose, as we desire to give the bees plenty of storage room.

Those hives only are suitable for extracting purposes which admit of tiering up one above the other. Such chambers may all be of one pattern; though with the stock hive only having standard frames, and that surmounted by successive stories of shallow frames, would be better. In either case use the empty chamber below, which will also to some extent prevent the queen ascending higher than the brood nest proper.

Perforated zinc is frequently recommended to keep the queen down, having slots $\frac{5}{32}$-inch wide, which presumably admit neither queen nor drones.

Deep hives, with the extra chamber for prevention of swarming, will rarely be left by the queen, and with the shallow extracting super, having its frames placed at right angles to those below, no adapter is needed.

All combs arranged for extracting should stand at a set distance apart all the time, as the surfaces will then be finished off evenly, thus making the uncapping process more rapid. Shallow combs are filled better than deep ones, and can be more readily manipulated.

Metal ends are used where frames are spaced at set distances, but none such are in use for extracting purposes, as then the frames should be farther apart—about $\frac{1}{4}$-inch more than usual.

Where there is any difficulty in restraining the queen, as where all shallow, or all standard frames may be used, if the queen excluder is objectionable, then place all succeeding sets of combs *below* the brood nest as recommended in Non-Swarming pamphlet.

Mr. Howard has designed single strips of excluder slots with plain $\frac{3}{8}$-inch sides, which can be inserted between the frame bars, thus spacing the frames at the same time, and being adapted to few or many frames.

## Spare Combs

for extracting may be obtained early in the season by inducing the bees to build out foundation (wired or otherwise), inserted in the brood nest; or later above it. The combs will be tougher, and a larger population will be obtained if such new combs remain in the hive for breeding purposes, while the outside older combs can be removed for storage.

With plenty of store combs and the " safety valve " below, the bees cannot well be idle if there is anything to be gathered. A common practice is to lift the upper storey and place another under, but where excluder zinc is used the brood nest is always retained at the bottom.

When removing completed sets, let it be done during the busy hours of the day, when what few bees are in will soon leave if piled up in a room with large windows arranged as explained under Bee-houses. Another way is to shake the bees from the combs, using a feather for the stragglers; and still another, with shallow frames when fixed securely, is that first adapted to modern hives by James Heddon, of Dowagiac, Mich., who had not the slightest knowledge that his " shaking out " process had been long practised in this country with fixed combs, where we call it " throwing."

Empty sets of combs must be in readiness to give the bees where more room may be required, and when full combs have been emptied, they should always be returned in the evening that all may be cleared up, and the consequent excitement subsided before another day's work commences.

## Bee-Traps

have been revived both at home and in America, under the name of bee-escapes and super clearers. Some fifteen years since these were much in vogue, but fell into disuse, as practical bee-keepers found they preferred, when once having raised the super, to clear it away at once, and it is not a little surprising

K

to find several advanced apiarists themselves entrapped into thinking there is anything to be gained by re-adopting this old and discarded fad.

Well, we have our stored combs in the outer honey house, and now they must go forward into the extracting room, having been cleared of bees.   We must first be sure that our

## Extracting Machine

is quite clean, and that it has been firmly secured in a suitable place, high enough that the honey may be run off into another large cylinder or tank, which again must have a treacle valve at a convenient height for drawing off.   The strainer must cover the entire mouth of the tank, and be placed directly under the valve of the extractor.   We now require an

## Uncapping Can

which is to be in two sections ; the upper part to receive the cappings, with a strainer at bottom and one or more bars of wood across the top whereon to stand the comb, while with the

## Uncapping Knife,

resting one end of the comb on the bars, and the upper end held by the projecting ear in the left hand, with the top bar towards you, with a slightly diagonal and sawing motion carry the knife from top to bottom, removing not only the cappings but all comb that may project beyond the plane of the frame ; reverse, and serve the opposite side in like manner, when the comb is to be inserted in one of the cages of the extractor with the top bar standing in a direction opposite to that in which the revolutions are to be made, as the cells inclining towards the top bar the honey leaves more readily.   Now, unless the

## Rate of Speed

be carefully regulated, the operator is liable to break his combs, and thus render them difficult to handle ; but by

Fig. 44.

Meadows' Tinned-back Extractor.

Fig. 43.

Stanley's Automatic Extractor (after Cowan).

turning slowly while emptying the first side the great weight of the other will not force the combs into the wire netting. Now reverse all combs, at first working at a slow pace, but gradually increasing the speed, until you may set the machine going as fast as it can be made to revolve, having already removed the bulk from the opposite sides, though with a steady motion. When at full speed, slip off the multiplying gear if on the horizontal pattern, when a great many revolutions will be made while you can go on uncapping. The combs should again be reversed, and the sides first done are to be rapidly turned round in the same way. In this manner no combs are damaged, while every drop of honey is obtained; and *most of the revolutions take place while the operator is uncapping the next set of combs.*

The idea of again using simple motion is creeping in, being recommended under some false notions of economy. In these days of competition we cannot afford to " creep " along at a snail's pace, and if we can do double the work in a given time, better and cleaner than the " slow-coach " method, surely we are threefold the gainers.

## Combs containing Brood

can be extracted from only in warm weather, when the speed required for the first side of heavy combs to prevent them breaking must not at any time be exceeded. With care, none of the larvæ will be displaced, and here again the multiplying gear will give the more even motion. It is safer to extract not at all from combs containing brood.

## Storage.

Our honey is running through the strainer, and presently the tank will be full; when it will be necessary to draw off and again strain into other receptacles, all of which must be convenient for filling smaller vessels as needed. In lieu of lids, the storage tanks must be covered with cloths carefully secured, when the honey will be more perfectly ripened, and after a few days it can be drawn off and will be remarkably clear, with the exception of two or three inches of the upper surface, which may be again strained and placed with other surface honey.   I have found no harm resulting from honey being stored in galvanized vessels, but where it may be required to stay for a considerable time, tanks should be of tin, though more expensive.

The produce of an apiary varies considerably in colour according to the plant it may be collected from, and each kind must be extracted and stored separately, as the different grades have varying values; while one kind may granulate more rapidly than another, and if all were mixed together the entire mass would soon follow the action of the smaller proportion.

### To prevent Granulation,

it is recommended that honey be heated to 190 degs. Fahr., and then corked up; nevertheless some kinds will granulate in spite of this.

### Crates

for bottles should be made to hold either one or three dozen, the latter being most useful, as being the extent of the more frequent order.  The divisions are best made of thin wood crossing and halved together, to form square recesses to take the bottles just tight.  (See Fig. 40.)

For tins little is needed except a plain strong box of the right depth to take a 6 lb., two 3 lbs., or three 2 lbs.; all of which must be of the same diameter, a point too often over-looked, but an advantage appreciated when packing a large number, and being able to use one-sized crate for all.

### Extractors.

The machine illustrated (Fig. 43) is of American make (Stanley's Automatic), in which the comb baskets are shewn to swing either way as required for emptying the reverse sides of the combs without removing them each time. The illustration is selected as presenting the uninitiated with a good idea of the manner in which extractors are made. The advertiser claims that it is the only one of the kind in the world ; but it is a matter of fact that Mr. T. W. Cowan was the inventor of the principle some years before the above was brought out ; his "Automatic" having gained many honours, and more recently this principle has been accredited to the inventor by prominent American apiarists.

However, there appears to be some objection made to these, as the parts are liable to get out of order, and many bee-keepers prefer the old style where the combs have to be lifted out each time they are reversed.

Mr. W. P. Meadows, of Syston, has introduced a very important improvement in extractors. As shown by Fig. 44, the wire cage against which the comb rests is itself backed by a sheet of tin ; the two being firmly fastened together, with an intervening space. The cage, or comb basket, is made incapable of bulging by strips of tin secured to the back at right angles to the same, and running from top to bottom ; thus permitting of a higher rate of speed without danger of breaking the combs. The extractor requires multiplying gear to make it more perfect, though a novice might certainly find it to his advantage to have an extractor wherewith he could not get up that excess of speed which would ruin his combs.

## Exhibition.

Extracted honey for show purposes must be bright and transparent, enclosed in a bottle having a screw cap, that the contents may be readily reached. The glass should be of the finest quality and the jar as narrow as possible.

Messrs. Abbott, of Southall, provide a very neat glass as Fig. 39, designed especially for exhibition purposes. The jar already mentioned, in 1 lb. and ½ lb. sizes, will also be found very suitable.

## COMB-HONEY.

So far many more people have gone in for producing this article than that in the liquid form ; consequently the price has gone down considerably during the past ten years.   It has fallen something like 6d. or 7d. per pound, whereas the other has come down about 2d.   It is time therefore that extracted honey had more attention if only to place comb at a better paying rate, as the latter has ruled too low until the past year or two.   Supply and demand, however, must regulate the price, and it is no use bee-keepers asking as much now as they obtained a few years since when the article was scarce, as wholesale and retail dealers alike are quite powerless to alter the state of the market.

The greater trouble, however, is that all the small producers throw their comb-honey upon the market as soon as it is removed from the hives, and thus a false impression is made, and prices rule low, accordingly, though the probability is that the total output may be under the average.

### Sections

have already been noticed in their various forms; and the kind one intends to adopt should be on hand before April 1st, when the foundation can be inserted during that month ; that all may be in readiness, as a flow of honey is liable to occur any time after May 1st, or even earlier.   In

### Preparing Stocks for Comb-Honey

it has been shewn under General Management that the brood nest should not be increased beyond the capacity of a ten or eleven-frame chamber of combs.   The hive may appear overcrowded, but while you are waiting for the honey flow, put on an upper storey and work out foundation, feeding as elsewhere shewn, for inserting in the sections.   It may be asked

## Why the Brood Nest should not be Extended

at this time ?   As a matter of fact, having already a complete brood nest, every day passing without an extension *adds a balance of power to the future working force* of the hive.   Extend the brood nest and you not only require a greater proportion of the stores to feed the young, but a larger number of the population is needed to attend to the enlarged nursery instead of adding to the stores.

It should be distinctly understood that it is not always the larger population which gives the heaviest surplus, as it is possible for the hive of medium strength to send out a much larger gathering force.   These are delicate points which require careful consideration but which are too often overlooked.

## An Exception

will be made where the plan of uniting is carried out prior to the honey flow, when for such doubled colonies two or more brood chambers must be allowed for the excess of numbers.

In this connection it may be mentioned that more often than not valuable queens of any prolific race are inserted at a time it is desirable an excess of brood should not be produced.   A black queen, or any one that has bred heavily during the early part of the season, is removed from a stock that is gathering abundantly and even crowding her out.   The young queen is inserted, and this being her first chance to enjoy her occupation, the stores rapidly give place to brood. The owner soon comes to the decision that the queen is too prolific and that her bees do nothing ; and yet the fault is simply his own.   That the same bees will gather honey as well or better than his original stock, he can at once prove for himself by simply removing the brood and giving empty combs, when he will in a short space of time see these combs as heavy with honey 'as the others were with brood (*see* page 50, on proper times for Queens to breed heavily).   Well, the

## First Honey Flow

is upon us ; weather steady, and temperature from 70° to 80° in the shade, with plenty of forage in all directions. Our sections are all ready on the hives, providing not less than 40 lbs. capacity with combs all drawn out ; or 20 lbs. to start with if only foundation is given, or with weaker colonies.

We are now in full working order, and in looking around we find here a hive and there another which require more surplus room, or the bees will be at work below the brood nest. Where any crates are completed remove them, inserting a fresh set in place of each. If foundation has to be used let that go next above the brood frames ; and combed sections if on hand are to be placed above those already on the hive. Great care must be taken to

## Reduce the Super-Space

towards the end of the season ; and this is done by gradually removing completed sections, and then closing up with the dummy. The open spaces thus left above the frames may be stopped by strips of wood or carpet. This plan is preferable to adding further sections, and the almost certainty of a great number being left incomplete.

An additional advantage is secured by this process of contraction as the season is closing. The bees are compelled to "crowd" on all the remaining comb space, and it does not appear to be generally known that while under this condition a far greater number of sections will be completed by the bees using honey carried up from the stock combs, even after gathering has actually ceased.

## Remove Sections

during the working hours of the day, when a few puffs of smoke will generally send all the bees below. If this fails, take out the combs one at a time and brush the bees off with a feather, first giving the section a shake ; but the operation must be rapidly carried out, because as soon as once frightened they will commence to tear open the beautifully capped cells, and it will therefore be seen that the sooner they are out the better. This too, is one of the most forcible arguments that can be used in condemnation of the super clearers, for the bees once frightened by the lifting of the super, will not hesitate to break countless pin holes in the beautiful cappings, more particularly when separated from the queen.

## Grading.

When brought in-doors every comb must be looked over, while at the same time all propolis or other stains are to be scraped off from the wood, taking care not to injure the face of the combs. All the whitest and best finished are to be first selected and stored in crates piled one over the other, with ventilation right through the whole tier. The next in order are those which, while being well finished, are not of such good colour. These are to be piled up fully exposed to the light and air for a time, when the colour will be equal to the first with which they may then be classed. If placed in crates for bleaching, the latter must stand singly or on end, so that the light may penetrate. A piece of strainer cloth or wire netting should take the place of the usual lid meanwhile, that there may be a free circulation of air.

What will constitute the second grade will be all that are not nicely finished, though there must not be too many incomplete cells. Those that are a little discolored can be restored as before. Any that cannot come in as second-rate must have their contents extracted and the combs stored for future use ; first making sure that no moisture remains about them by placing a number over any strong stock towards evening, when the bees will soon clean them.

## The Store Room

should be perfectly dry, thoroughly ventilated, having a con-
crete floor, and all so carefully arranged that neither mice,
bees, nor other insects can gain admission. (For further
particulars see Bee-houses, &c.)

## Preparing for Market.

Crates can be made to hold anything from one to three
dozen, the latter being mostly required. It is imperative that
there be glass on each side parallel with the face of the combs,
not only to make the package more attractive, but as the
greatest safeguard against rough handling. As an additional
protection against friction, the sides and bottoms should be
lined with patent corrugated paper, when there will be little
fear of breakages.

Though more expensive, the crate may be placed on a
false bottom with coiled springs, of a power necessary to resist
the weight that is to be placed above.

Sections should be enclosed in clean white paper, pasted
securely where overlapping, when if any breakage does occur,
the contents of the damaged one will not escape and spoil
others.

The above should be done with each section, whether fancy
boxes are used or not, but while the latter additional expense
may do if retailed at home, it will certainly not pay at wholesale. I have obtained as much for sections without as others
were getting with fancy boxes, in the same town ; one should
therefore be very careful before adding this expense to his
commodity.

Section holders introduced by Mr. Woodleigh have been
used largely, and will no doubt be more appreciated in the
future. They are made of tin, folding somewhat like the
American section, and will be found very durable, as, if soiled,
they can be readily cleaned. They can be had in several

colours, and though expensive in the first instance, that is not a very serious consideration, seeing they can be used many times without injury.

## Selling Honey.

Where the apiarist retails his honey, of course he will always have his own label on it; something as neat and attractive as possible. It is surprising what a number of bee-keepers there are who will send from 100 to 500 lbs. of honey to a distant town at a very much lower rate than could be obtained at retail near home, if only a little perseverance were used. This shows a great want of business tact, in thus depriving themselves and injuring producers at large by reducing the value of their crop.

In securing some efficient tradesman to handle honey, where one has a large quantity, some difficulty will be experienced at times, as there are many who will not put it forward. If a grocer himself owns bees, *his* honey is very soon passed over the counter; and why not that of others where the grocer is not following the pursuit? Perhaps the fault is with the price, but, nevertheless, being a comparatively new article the retailer must be induced to take a lively interest in it. Make it attractive by providing a good show case, and cards; and let him have a consignment "on sale or return" to start with, and there is no doubt he will soon send for more. Do not attempt to send any without complete protection from flies, &c., as this is one of the most frequent objections made against having it in stock.

## For Exhibition,

Combs must be visible on both sides, using for the purpose only those sections of the very best colour and finish. In some quarters it has been considered that the comb should not be sealed close to the wood all round, but this is a serious error,

the idea being that the section can be more easily cut out; but
I have yet to find the retailer who does not prefer those for his
window which are sealed perfectly all round the edges; and
when one of each may be placed on the scale, is there a doubt
as to which the customer would select ?　Moreover, those that
are filled close up to the wood will stand the risk of transit far
better than would otherwise be the case.

CHAPTER XV.

# QUEEN REARING.

I T should be understood that when a colony is deprived of its queen the bees are soon aware of the loss, and forth-with special cells are constructed upon larvæ that may be from one to three or four days old, but very seldom are *eggs* selected in such a case of emergency. In due time a queen is hatched from one of such cells, and though she may have enjoyed the usual quantity of royal jelly, it frequently happens that the first to emerge from her cradle is one that is not well developed, as the oldest larvæ would naturally come soonest to maturity. Thus those which had been selected from the egg, or one or two days after hatching therefrom, and would have received only the royal food from the first day of their existence, and consequently are destined to be perfect in formation, are sacrificed to a dwarfed and ill-formed queen.

As already shewn, only one of the queens is reserved, though several may be raised. There are two points, therefore, of importance to the bee-keeper who wishes to obtain a number of queens. The colony that is to produce them must either be made queenless, or be maintained at a swarming condition ; and then he is to guard against the destruction of the surplus queens.

### The Plan often Recommended,

and that only recently in the *British Bee Journal*, of simply removing a queen from a colony in normal condition and then inducing the bees to start queen cells where desired by enlarging the mouth of worker cells, is really more simple than practical. In the first place, one cell only is never large enough to form the base of a queen cell; two at least are thrown into one, but more often three; and where the bees have unlimited material at hand a queen cell will not be built upon one in fifty of such enlarged cells. I have had the proof of this assertion in my own apiary, and where Ligurians are concerned very often only two or three cells are started. One of

## My own Plans

is to remove the queen and all the brood combs with adhering bees from a crowded hive, and place them in a new situation, with the exception of those shaken from two combs, into the old hive, when with the flying bees a fair swarm will be obtained. Next, go to the hive containing the queen you desire to breed from and look up the comb of eggs, or such just hatching by preference, and in a warm room cut the comb asunder from end to end, horizontally at about one-third of its depth from the top bar. Now along *each side* of the lower edge of the septum make vertical incisions with the point of a penknife, cutting away the cell walls in the shape of the letter V inverted. Do not cut so close to the base as to displace the eggs, and let the incisions be made about $\frac{1}{4}$-inch apart. Our cells will generally be built from these hollow spaces, and though not perfectly regular it is seldom that any two are joined together.

The reader may be tempted to put the whole comb in just as he takes it from the hive, or simply as sliced asunder, but only to find that he will not get one cell in five, and those not so regular as with the V-cuts. The remainder of the comb may be cut into strips and fastened into other frames in like manner, but unless the bees are very numerous it is not desirable to put more than one prepared comb into one hive at a time. I have used frames with parallel bars and strips

Fig. 45.
Comb prepared for
Queen Rearing.

Fig. 46.
Queen Nursery (on end)
for Top of Hive.

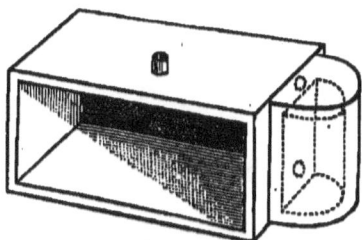

Fig. 47.
Tin Boiler for Queen Lamp Nursery.

Fig. 48.
Tubular Virgin Queen Cage.

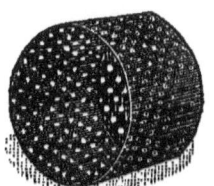

Fig. 49.
Circular Queen Cage.

of comb with eggs on each, but find nothing more simple and practical than the one piece, which gives from ten to twenty cells at a time.

By the time the prepared comb is ready the broodless and queenless bees will have found out their loss, and being greatly excited are in the best condition possible for starting queen cells. Place a comb or two of stores at each side, and after two or three days add combs of hatching brood to keep up a population of young bees.

## Another Method

frequently adopted with great success in my own apiary is that of selecting combs heavily charged with brood on the point of hatching with all the adhering bees—using one from each of eight or nine good colonies, taking care not to remove either queen. Place these combs in a new hive which for convenience should have been carried round in collecting them, and after a few hours, or next day, insert the prepared comb of just hatching larvæ near to the centre. The young bees thus congregated (of course, well provided with stored combs of *unsealed* honey and pollen) will produce some of the finest queens ever seen. Remove all queen cells that may be started on others than the prepared frame and add other combs of brood just being capped, so that later on as many good nuclei as possible may be made up.

## The Cell Nursery.

Where a large number of queens are required, as soon as any queen cells are capped, they are to be removed with adhering bees to another queenless hive retained for this express purpose.

Mark each frame with the date of setting the eggs, and allow eleven days before cutting out the cells, that they may remain in the correct temperature of the hive until the last, and yet be certain that none hatch to cause mischief.

Our cells, therefore, are not removed until the queens are almost at maturity, and now they are to be placed in the

## Queen Nursery.

This may consist of a shallow frame composed of a number of compartments 1½-inch wide with a wire loop in one side to hold the cell. Place this frame on top of the cell nursery hive with a piece of linen intervening ; the lower side of the frame is to be covered with a piece of ticking, glued to the partition walls, and the top of each compartment is to be covered with a piece of wire cloth. (Fig. 46.) For this purpose, the sides of the hive should project above the frames so that the heat may be retained, and the whole is to be covered first by a layer of felt, next a sheet of American oil cloth, and again one or more pieces of felt. The entire heat of the hive is thus reserved, and the temperature of the nursery will be about 90°. It should not descend below 85° nor rise above 95°, and must be carefully regulated by the size of the entrance, in accordance with the outside temperature. This plan will be found far preferable to those nurseries hanging in the hive like an ordinary frame, as the temperature is more certain, and one can see at a glance when a queen has hatched ; it is useless, however, to place the nursery over any but the most powerful colony.

Where one does not mind handling the bees more frequently, the best plan that can possibly be devised is to use the cage, Fig. 49, which is placed over queens or queen cells, where both honey and pollen is to be seen in the cells; in this case the queens need little attention, and always feed in the most natural manner. Where hatched in other nurseries they should at once be placed over natural stores in this manner, as no other plan of feeding them will compensate for the loss of pollen.

## The Lamp Nursery

is frequently used and is invaluable for hatching queens. It consists of double walls and bottom of tin, with stays inside to keep the water from bulging out the sides; and the internal capacity is large enough to take some half-dozen brood frames, with plenty of lateral space to spare. What might be added with benefit are small holes punched through near the upper inner margin of the tin wall to give moisture. The lid must be of wood covered with warm material, and if the whole is cased in wood, with the exception of an opening above the lamp, the temperature will be more even, and a very small flame will suffice to keep the chamber at about 90°, the boiler being filled in the first place with water at about 100°. The frames are placed in as the cells near maturity, and the young queens are removed as fast as they gnaw their way out ; several visits daily being required, as they are liable to destroy each other and tear open the other cells as soon as their strength is gained. For the first few hours, however, they can do little harm.

The lamp nursery is sometimes objected to as being *unnatural.* Where is reason, if we allow such ill-founded statements to influence our actions ? Are our processes of queen-raising natural ? Is our entire management natural ? No ! only in so far that natural conditions do not interfere with greater profits. Let me ask those who use the hanging-frame nursery if they have observed the temperature surrounding a queen cell with the bees always packed closely around it, thus giving greater or at least more certain heat than is required for the rest of the hive ? If so, they will be surprised to find how much lower is the temperature surrounding cells where no bees can cluster upon them, and where they do not even care to crowd upon the metal at each side of the little cages so many apiarists use in hanging-frames. All animal life is produced by heat, varying according as the nature of the creature may require, and for our purpose the lamp nursery supplies the correct and even temperature desired.

The illustration, Fig. 47, gives the metal portion of my own queen nursery, an apparatus I had made in the first instance as an incubator for chickens' eggs. The rectangular portion shows the opening at the side, with a double casing on all other sides, with about 1-inch between the inner and outer walls.   The whole of this compartment is enclosed by wood with a closely-fitting door which closes the said open side. The inside is fitted with skeleton framework wherein slide several drawers, each covered on the underside with woven wire.   The same arrangement will also take whole frames of comb, but I prefer to have the cells built that they may be cut out singly and so placed in the trays.   A thermometer lies on the centre division of one of the drawers ; while another is fixed in a vertical position under glass in the centre of the door ; this glass being again covered by a close fitting shutter to avoid extremes; thus the internal temperature can be noted at a glance without exposing the cells.   With my arrangement, however, the heat is always given from above, and even after examination of the interior there is not the same loss of heat as with the nurseries hitherto used where the whole top is opened, as such have no large body of heat just where most needed for the immediate restoration of the correct temperature.

Though shown at one end, the hollow heating cylinder H C is at the centre of the back.   Under this is placed the lamp, which has a wick of such a size than it cannot very well have a flame which will overheat the chamber ; the latter being about 18 inches by 12 inches by 9 inches.   The boiler contains between the walls about six gallons of water, so that when the right temperature is once secured it does not vary one degree in twelve hours.   The whole stands upon legs with a small table for the lamp to rest upon ; this is trimmed once in twenty-four hours, regularly every evening, so that there is no chance for the flame to drop during the night, when no attention is needed.   Any cells expected to hatch may have the point passed into the tubular perforated cages, as used for inserting virgin queens, Fig. 48, thus obviating the constant attention otherwise necessary.

A sponge or cloth saturated with water, or a shallow tray holding a small quantity, should be placed in the chamber to induce the necessary moisture. The outer casing of wood has a movable lid, not very tight fitting ; but between it and the boiler several folds of flannel are laid, thus permitting a gradual change of air to take place in the cell chamber without loss of heat. A tin plate is placed under the bottom to guard against fire, an opening, of course, corresponding with that in the hollow cylinder.

Though the time of hatching is delayed under a temperature of 85°, I find queens will come out with perfect wings, but I prefer it regulated nearly as possible at 90° rather than 95°, so that in case of any accident there may be no danger resulting from either extreme. When properly managed, no intelligent apiarist will deny that the incubator or lamp nursery gives a more even temperature than can be obtained in the hive. That of the former is almost perfect, while the hive varies considerably, having its entrance always open to the outer air.

We have provided for the hatching of our queens, and must now prepare for their reception in

## Nuclei.

These are small hives to hold from three to six frames, the latter being more serviceable for our purpose, as there is room to add fresh combs of brood when necessary.

It seldom happens that good nuclei can be made up from a stock which at the time has its queen, therefore my own plan is in the first place to make up a nucleus with the queen of the most suitable colony, being one very populous, having a number of combs with hatching brood in each. Place this queen with one frame of brood and bees, and enough more to cover two other combs, on a new stand. On the third day thereafter make up further nuclei in like manner from the same hive, leaving the younger brood in the original hive, as there will be plenty of bees to take care of the same. Bearing in mind they have already lost their queen and having prepared for building queen cells, no further excitement will take place, and not one-fourth the number of bees will return to the old hive, as when the nuclei are drawn from one with a queen presiding.

Insert the young queens the same evening by allowing them to run in direct, or place them in my

## Virgin Queen Cage,

Fig. 48, which is a small tube of finely perforated tin or zinc, about ½-inch in diameter and 2 inches long, one end being stopped with the same material; and after the queen is placed in, the open end is pressed into super foundation, when with a slight turn a piece is cut out which completely stops the opening. The cage is now carried to the nucleus and inserted between the upper part of two combs, wax end downwards. The young queen soon bites her way out, just as she has done from her natural cradle. The cage should be passed down so as to bruise the cappings of honey to ensure that she is well provided for, and as she will then partake of the same honey as the workers it is all in her favour. The best time for inserting them being the evening; and when a laying queen is removed, the young one to follow must not be inserted until the second day after.

We shall probably have

## Surplus Virgin Queens,

and where these cannot be accommodated by breaking up other stocks, one-frame nuclei must be on hand provided with thorough ventilation, and in which are to be placed a comb of stores (both honey and pollen), with three or four hundred bees. These may be side combs from nuclei already established, and should contain no brood.

After the confined bees have been in an uproar for a short time, having already made provision for a small opening, allow the young queen to run in. Keep these in. a dark room and use as needed in outside nuclei.

It has been observed that a young queen feeds upon pollen extensively until she has met the drone, from which time she is fed by the bees entirely upon digested food. Now, just here, I wish to show the

### Folly of keeping Young Queens confined

in the frame nurseries for a number of days after hatching, as is done extensively, especially in several American queen-raising apiaries.

Without the nitrogenous food at this time, when their constitutions should be established, they are dragging out their existence upon sugar alone at the most important period of their growth. The editor of the *American Bee Journal* has repeatedly given his voice against the cheap queen traffic, and is it any wonder when they are produced wholesale with constitutions thus impaired?

By all means let us have cheap queens—they have been far too high in price, though unavoidably so hitherto, for the general benefit; but we do not want them produced without due regard to the laws of re-production.

The confined one-frame nucleus certainly takes up more space and time, but both are amply paid for by getting more substantial stock, while queens being able to feed naturally will get mated sooner than those with a weakened frame.

On p. 50 it will have been noticed that for

### Supplying all Hives with Young Queens*

yearly, and to compensate for the non-increase of stocks, one colony in ten is to be devoted to increase by nuclei. In this case, the tenth hives are to be stimulated for brood rearing until the end of June, when there should be at least three chambers nearly full of brood in all stages. However, to be

---

* Simmins' Non-Swarming System, Feb., 1886.

within limit, we will say twenty combs of brood and a number of stored and partly-stored combs.

The whole tier should now be shifted to a new location, one storey at a time, and then give the swarm (made as before) the eggs for queen raising ; this time an upper storey of combs or foundation is to be added, besides filling up below, as the much larger number of bees will probably store heavily. The moved stock will still have sufficent bees to care for the brood, the extent of which will now be immensely increased, as there are not enough gatherers left to crowd the queen out, though before shifting the hive the apiarist should have been able to give the queen plenty of room by alternating brood combs with foundation as the upper storeys were added, and extracting if necessary.

On the ninth day after setting the eggs, make up a nucleus with the queen (of the moved lot), this time standing the same by the hive, to be returned after forming the nuclei in a manner similar to that before mentioned, standing a nucleus by each of the full hives working for honey, to be united to them in the autumn.

By waiting till the date named more than sufficient nuclei can be made up, while the original queen will have a full hive of bees to build up with again, and thus provide against loss, and have combs of eggs to spare for the nuclei.

## The Young Queens

may be mated from after their seventh day until they are as much as four weeks old. In fair weather, the rule is for them to be laying in ten or eleven days from hatching ; but through unfavorable weather, I have had a number of queens under the closest observation failing to mate until the twenty-eighth day, and then successfully, having seen them come in with the drone attachment and in due course produce properly capped brood. I have had many mated at twenty-one to twenty-five days.

However, when a queen gets much beyond fourteen days, it requires the most sunny and calm day to enable her to become successful in securing a mate, though such days are, of course, always desirable. Young and vigorous queens will occasionally fly at an opportune moment, and become successful in somewhat windy weather. But the temperature must not be low. It is only under a high temperature with little or no wind that general success is attained where queens are reared on a large scale.

Nuclei should be constantly renovated by the addition of fresh brood, whether they are to be soon united or not ; and they should always be in possession of stored combs, in preference to any form of daily feeding, other than Simmins' dry feeders.

## Eggs for Queen Raising

are more readily obtained from our select queens if the latter are in small colonies, having not more than four combs well crowded with bees, and protected at the sides with chaff dummies. When a comb of eggs is removed, at the same operation insert another, empty, or a sheet of foundation if not too late in the season. Continue the process every two or three days if many queens are being reared, with a number of such hives to keep up the supply ; and where it is likely that too much honey will be brought in to hinder the queen by the little lot getting strong, then carry the queen and two or three of the best combs of brood and accompanying bees to a new situation, thus providing her with attendants mostly too young to store a surplus. Use the remainder as a nucleus, or add to another hive.

## Drones

are to be produced by stock which has shown good qualities and correct colour (if pure) for two generations back, as the colony directly producing them does not impart to our drones its own characteristics. For their good qualities we must look to the grand-parent, and the colony producing the drone which

mated with her, if possible.   Early drones are best secured by
arranging drone comb at the centre of a well-provided stock
the previous autumn.   No useless drones should be produced
as they consume considerable stores.   A strong colony, well
provided and made queenless in autumn before the slaughter
is likely to commence, will save their drones till winter, but
the special breeding of drones for autumn work must be.
carried on during July!

CHAPTER XVI.

# INTRODUCTION OF ALIEN QUEENS TO STOCKS.

NEXT to Queen Rearing, one of the most interesting features in connection with modern Bee-keeping is that of inserting queens, that they may preside over another colony with which hitherto they have had no relation. At first sight, therefore, it would appear that the bees will not hesitate to destroy the stranger; under some conditions this is the case, and various ways have been devised to guard against this disposition of theirs. The different methods come under two distinct systems: the old, called "Caging," and the new, known as " Simmins' Direct Introduction."

Generally speaking, the caging process is carried out by placing the queen in a small perforated compartment, wherein she is confined between two combs among the bees for forty-eight hours, when the bee-keeper opens the hive carefully and allows the queen to run among her new subjects. If then attacked, she must be again confined, and tried after the lapse of another twelve hours.

Direct Introduction consists in so inserting the queen without confinement that the bees are either unaware of the new arrival, or are taken advantage of in such a manner that they do not attempt to molest her.

Of course it is understood that no other queen is to be in the hive at the time another is to be given, or the new one will certainly be destroyed.    The novice may experience some difficulty in

## Finding the Queen

to be superseded, and he will certainly do better to leave his queens alone until he gains more experience, unless he is absolutely certain that any are actually failing.    If he tries any new race, as yet he is hardly capable of forming a correct opinion of them, and the probability is that the natives will answer his purpose best for the first year or two at least.

In frame hives the fertile queen can generally be found without much trouble, as she is parading the brood combs, the hive being opened with as little disturbance as possible, and the frames gently lifted and examined one by one.    If not to be seen there, look well around the edges of the combs, or she may be found on the floor, or at one corner among the bees : it may even be necessary to remove the combs to a temporary hive while looking for her around the sides, taking care not to get the brood chilled.    An unfertile or virgin queen is often most difficult to find, and at times even an expert bee-keeper would be tempted to say that no queen was there, were it not that the actions of the bees tend to show otherwise.    A careful examination will generally reveal her presence ; but failing to find her, when you think there should be one, give the bees a comb of unsealed brood, and if they build queen cells thereon it is almost certain no queen is there ; if otherwise, do not risk the life of a valuable queen until the other has been found. With fixed combs the only way is to "drive" the bees out and catch the queen as she ascends.    If that cannot be done, then look well among the deserted combs and the bees clustering in the empty skep.    The length of the body, as well as its brighter color, should enable one to distinguish the royal form, while it should be remembered that the queen's legs are always of a reddish brown color, those of the workers being much darker.

## INTRODUCTION BY CAGING.

Procure a cage made of fine perforated zinc 1½-inch in diameter, and 1-inch deep, having one end only closed with the same material. When the queen arrives place her in this cage while yet indoors, slip a thin card under and carry her to the hive. Without removing the frames other than to give plenty of room laterally, slide the cage carefully from the card on to uncapped cells of honey, within the margin of the cluster, and press it down to the mid-rib of the comb with a cutting motion. The queen now has plenty of food, and if the perforations are fine enough the bees are unable to molest her. After forty-eight hours, give a puff or two of smoke, carefully examine the condition of the bees nearest the cage, and if simply passing their tongues through the perforations, the queen may be released without fear of the bees attacking her, but all the same watch their actions closely for a few moments. If all is well the bees will gather around her, but not thickly; those nearest will clean her with their tongues, while one or two may be seen feeding her. Under that condition the hive may be closed and left, but should they be found clustering tightly in large numbers about the cage, at once close the hive and wait another twelve hours; and in case a queen is attacked after being released (which is known by the bees forming into a knot about her and stinging each other in their endeavour to so do to the stranger, called "balling"), then confine her again, first dispersing the angry cluster by heavy smoking.

When inserting queens by caging, it is necessary to keep all queen cells destroyed, or the new-comer will seldom be received. She is to them unserviceable, and yet present in the hive all the time the bees know they have the means of raising their own, and hence a dislike once began is only fed into an angry flame simply by the continued irritation caused by the constant attempt to get at the stranger, and not seldom by the bee-keeper's own interference.

Under this process of frequent disturbance, the queen

will sometimes even herself be the first to attack the bees, and then, of course, there is no hope for her if not again confined. All these misfortunes are brought about through the necessity of operating by daylight, but there are one or two other methods which do not necessitate so much manipulation. The " Raynor " cage, consisting of a narrow and long wire cage, can be passed down between two combs from the feed hole in quilt (if one), while with a wire rod connected with a small hinged plate at the bottom, the operator can, after the usual lapse of time, release the queen without opening the hive. I must here add what I know to be an improvement :—*Release the queen after darkness has set in*, on the night of the same day she is inserted.

Mr. Cheshire places a flat cage on (not cut into) the capped brood, where it is held by a spring passed over the top bar, when in the course of a few hours the bees cut a passage under the edge of the cage, and thus liberate the queen without further disturbance. For greater security let me advise something more definite : *Put the queen in towards evening, so that she may be liberated of a certainty during the quiet hours of the night.*

Though there are many methods of caging, I will call attention to only one more, which is deserving of some notice. Mr. G. M. Doolittle, an American bee-keeper, uses a flat cage, having an area of 4 or 5 inches square; this, with the queen in, is pressed down to the mid-rib of the comb just over hatching brood. Of course all the young bees hatching out pay homage to the only queen they know; and the cells thus vacated are occupied by eggs laid by the confined queen. By this time there is not much doubt about the queen being accepted by the rest of the population, and she may be released. In this case it is evident that food must be present, therefore see that the cage also takes in an inch or more of sealed store. Where food is given to a queen confined in the " Raynor," " Cheshire," or any other cage, *honey from the same hive should alone be supplied*; and on no account may any of the bees which accompanied her be placed in the cage; but it is advisable to give her an escort of some half-dozen young workers picked from the comb just after hatching, and taken from the hive in which the queen is to be caged. By these methods the most favourable time for inserting queens is during the months when they are breeding and storing; but in autumn the bees are more inclined to resent intrusion, where so much disturbance is necessary.

## DIRECT INTRODUCTION.

A term first applied by myself in the year 1881, will be found much more simple than the foregoing, in that it enables the bee-keeper to insert a queen without loss of time and by two of my own methods to any colony, at any time of the year, whatever be the condition of the hive, whether it contains queen cells up to the point of hatching, brood in every stage of development, fertile workers, or no brood at all.

### Simmins' "Comb Method,"

first brought to public notice by my pamphlet in 1881, consists in taking a queen from a nucleus, or otherwise, upon the comb she is parading among her own bees, and then inserting the whole into the desired hive, using a little smoke as in ordinary manipulation. Be careful to carry the comb in an *uncovered* box from nucleus to full colony, and before inserting the same, part the combs of the hive to give plenty of room and admit light. (*See also* " Uniting.")

### Simmins' " Fasting Method,"

long since practised by myself and first mentioned in the pamphlet upon Direct Introduction, I have since improved by inserting the queen at night. The three things of importance to be observed are as follows:—(1) Keep the queen quite alone for not less than thirty minutes; (2) she is to be without food meanwhile; (3) and to be allowed to run down from the top of

M

the frames after darkness has set in, by lamplight.   It is also important that the same receptacle be not used twice over for holding the queen during the thirty minutes' probation without first being scalded or otherwise cleansed.   Of course a metal cage is easily made clean, though there is no objection to the cheap " safety " match boxes so commonly in use, as there is nothing obnoxious about this kind.   My own practice is to carry the queens in the vest pockets, in small tubular cages made of fine perforated zinc or tin, one end permanently closed, while the other end is pressed into a piece of foundation after the queen is in.   When ready, remove the foundation and let her run into the hive.   Caution:—Make no examination after inserting a queen, by either of the two foregoing plans, until 48 hours have expired.

The above meets all requirements, whether the colony has been long, or only a short time queenless ; if it has brood or not, or queen cells in any stage of development.   It is also applicable to any season of the year.

## Mr. Pond's Method.

Mr. J. E. Pond, jun., an American apiarist, gives his method as follows : Remove the old queen about mid-day, and towards evening, or when the bees have ceased working for the day, let the new queen run into the entrance.   He says it is important that the queen be inserted the same day.   It would appear that the interval named gives the bees time to discover their loss, and thus provides them with another queen when they feel most inclined to accept one, just before making any serious attempt to raise one of their own.   The plan is, however, not so successful as when the queen is first confined alone, without food, and then inserted after darkness has set in.

## Introduction by Chloroform,

puffball, &c., is sometimes recommended, but I cannot advise such a course as to reduce the bees to a state of stupefaction, being not only injurious but totally unnecessary. Mr. D. A. Jones, late Editor of *The Canadian Bee Journal*, formerly a great advocate of this method, has discarded it in favour of my Fasting plan, which he now considers the most satisfactory.

## Covering Queens with Honey.

It is claimed by some that a queen is generally accepted if first covered with honey and then placed among the bees; but the practice is one of doubtful utility; in the first place, there is no restriction as to *what* honey, and if any desire to try the plan, I must say that no other honey should be used but what is then and there taken from the hive the queen is to be dropped into. An ordinary pocket knife can be used to scoop out a little honey from the capped cells ; or failing that, use the same syrup that is being fed to the bees. The body of the bee is studded with breathing tubes ; it is, therefore, evident that much mischief, if not permanent injury, is caused by all being clogged with honey, if only for a few minutes.

## Running Queen and Bees in at the Entrance.

Another method sometimes recommended, but long since tried and discarded by myself, is this :—Shake all the bees from the combs on to a board in front of the hive, and as they draw back through the entrance let the new queen run in with them. There is considerable risk with this plan, even when all are sprayed with thin syrup, scented or not, but I mention it more as a caution to the novice, that he may not be led astray, particularly as he would be liable to get the brood chilled before the bees regained their former position.

## Simmins' Nucleus Method.

A plan which I have found very satisfactory, and which was first suggested to my mind by the fact that I had long made a practice of sending queens off with bees they had never seen until the moment of fastening down in the various receptacles they were to travel in, is as follows :—Make up a 3-frame nucleus in a small hive 14½ inches by 11 inches inside (allowing 2½ inch space under the "standard" frame); then confine the bees, with ample ventilation, and as soon as they are in an uproar, having found themselves to be queenless, let the new arrival run under one corner of the quilt, first driving the bees back with a little smoke. Keep them thus confined in a darkened room, and liberate on the evening of the third day, standing the nucleus where it is to remain ; and as soon as strong enough give a frame of hatching brood at intervals of seven days. Before inserting queen, she should, for greater security, be kept alone and without food for 30 minutes.

Mr. Doolittle (of America) also appears to have discovered that confined bees will readily accept a strange queen. His plan is to shake the bees into a box, well ventilated, and as soon as they are in distress at the loss of their queen, he allows the new one to run among them through a small opening, otherwise kept closed. In a day or two the bees are placed upon brood and store combs, where it is intended they shall remain.

Few bees will return to the old hive in either case, but there appears to be more labour than with my own plan, in that bees are twice shaken from the combs; first to place them in confinement, and next to provide the brood and other combs to start them in a new situation. By my plan, the bees have their own combs all the time, and when liberated the same have already been largely stocked with eggs by the new queen.

## Colonies long Queenless.

When I am aware a colony has been queenless for any length of time, I generally take out one of the central combs and allow the queen to run among the bees ; if favourably received, replace the comb, but if, as it seldom happens, they reject her, then give them a frame of honey and brood, and insert the queen at night according to the "fasting" method.

In times of scarcity it is always better to have the feeding-bottle going when it is decided to insert a queen by any caging process.

All the foregoing plans have reference to fecundated queens, but with regard to the introduction of

## Virgin Queens,

hitherto there has been great uncertainty, and the only satisfactory plans I have found are :—(1) By introducing to a confined nucleus as shewn above for fertile queens ; (2) by the tubular cage before mentioned ; in this case pressing the open end into *thin* foundation after putting in the young queen ; and (3) by allowing three days to pass after the removal of a fertile queen, and then inserting at night. (*See also* Queen Rearing.)

## Queens Dying in Cage.

When inserting queens by the cage it sometimes happens that they are found dead. This results from one of two causes : either want of food, or death by stinging or worrying, as the perforations are too large in almost all cages used. The former shows the danger of using such cages as do not press into the combs, should the bees be disinclined to feed the stranger ; while the latter evil can be remedied by using perforations no larger than an ordinary pin will pass. We may now, indeed, consider the period of uncertainty, as in the days of queen caging, to have passed away. Under the author's own management, the subject of queen introduction has been reduced to a certainty. In addition to the methods of direct introduction, already enumerated, the experience gained by an extensive practice has resulted in the following additional observations, which must prove of service to many who may have cause to introduce queens.

A fertile queen is rarely objected to where queen cells are already capped over, and one may be run in at any time of the day.

Any such colony will also accept a virgin queen right away, and if broken up into nuclei the respective divisions will accept one or more unfertilised queens.

Upon the removal of a virgin queen, a fertile one will almost certainly be accepted if inserted at once; or any other virgin queen will be treated equally as well.

A colony deprived of the queen and the whole of its brood will accept either a virgin or fertile queen as soon as they are in an uproar because of such loss. The absence of the queen is detected almost immediately when the brood also is removed. Many bees are lost if bees are allowed to remain thus deprived for any length of time. My first Holy Land queen was introduced in this way fifteen years since, and though there is some trouble in removing the brood, I have always found the plan reliable, and the bees humming merrily, in possession of a new queen, within an hour of the removal of their own queen and brood.

## The Loss of Valuable Queens

has frequently been deplored, and yet the persons attempting the introduction went at it in a most clumsy way, especially when we consider that better and more certain methods were known to them. Valuable or other queens need not be lost if only the most simple precautions are taken. For instance, absolute safety can be ensured by removing a frame of hatching brood from a hive, and after shaking off all the adult bees, this brood comb placed in a narrow nucleus box will soon produce many hundreds of young bees who of a necessity will do homage to the only queen they know. The box can be stood in a hot-house for a few days, or hot water bottles can be kept going on either side, and within a week another like comb can be added and full liberty given by placing the nucleus in the permanent hive. Food should be present while confinement lasts, and a supply continued if the weather is not favorable.

## Simmins' Direct Introduction Proved.

It is only in the ordinary course of human nature that my very successful system of direct introduction should have some envious detractors ; but a more extravagant statement than that made by one bee-keeper can hardly be imagined. It was to the effect that while he admitted " the queens would be safely introduced, they would not lay for many days, and the bees paid them no attention, consequently, in a short time a number were thrown out of the hive."

In his eagerness to condemn the system he only shewed the more plainly his own ignorance of the nature and habits of bees. It is no fault of the system, if he experimented only with aged queens, or, on the other hand, inserted virgin queens, which, failing to mate, turned out useless, or were lost because of unsuitable weather for them to fly and become fertilised. Strange, indeed, he does not know that if a queen is once accepted she is at once treated as the reigning queen, and no amount of specious reasoning to the contrary can alter the fact.

Why is it, in my own case, my queens go on to lay *at once*, and remain in the respective hives month after month, and are only removed when sold, it may be one, two, or twelve months thereafter ?

And why should numerous correspondents write as follows : " I have inserted thirty queens by your method and all have been successful and done well " ? The number may be more or less, but the unsolicited testimonials must have some element of truth in them ! Note Mr. D. A. Jones' statement, already given. Surely the bee-king of Canada would not favor the method if it only meant loss of queens !

Who has once read Mr. F. Cheshire's testimony in his valuable work, and can for a moment doubt the value of my

system ?   " Following up the question, I tried many dozens of experiments, and found that by Mr. Simmins' method it was quite easy, and not only to introduce, but to get one queen *to lay* in half-a-dozen distinct hives in a single week.  .  .  .  . My trials have, I believe, embraced almost every supposable difficulty and variation in season and in the condition of the stocks, and show the system to be practically perfect.  .  .  .
. . Direct introduction, as taught by Mr. Simmins, has saved me queens, time, and anxiety, and I feel pleasure in expressing my indebtedness."

Yet other evidence is given by the editor of the *Beekeeper's Record* of Dec. 1st, 1887.   After detailing his experience in inserting by my method seven queens " at a season and under circumstances such as made us formerly careful to an extreme, we are glad to be able to pronounce the method a complete success.  .  .  .  . We can now understand how friend Simmins is able to guarantee safe introduction for queens sold by him, and we rejoice at being able to chronicle another point gained."

The foregoing statements will show the value of the system as applied to varying conditions of the bees, or the seasons, and as the editor of the *Record* himself says, " The introducing cage bids fair to be relegated to our collection of curiosities."

## CHAPTER. XVII

# INCREASE, AND ITS RELATION TO PROFITS.

EXCEPT in the few districts where the season is protracted, increase is obtained at the expense of honey; but in any case it is not desirable to take more than one swarm from the old stock; and this division to give the best results should be made either before the first honey-flow occurs, providing the colony can be made strong at that time, or during July, when little work is generally being carried on by the bees in most districts. But, that we may allow for uniting in the autumn, it will be safe to reckon only upon 50 per cent. increase, as it is imperative that all be kept in good condition. In the table of estimates this has been placed at a much lower rate, so that there is little fear of the apiarist weakening his stock.

A division of stocks can also be made during any interval of dearth, if not too late in the season, but in any case a young queen should be on hand. The operation of

## Dividing      .

will consist in removing from a strong colony one half of the brood combs containing mostly hatching brood, with the bees clustering thereon, as well as the queen; placing these in a new location, with all the brood near the centre of the hive with empty combs or foundation on either side of the same. The brood combs remaining on the old stand are to be alternated with foundation, as the larger number of bees will be here, and on the evening of the third day following, unite with them the nucleus having a young queen, or insert the queen alone if the nucleus is again required. The reason for waiting three days in this case is solely because of the bees returning from the removed portion which may not always be friendly to the queen which they know is not the one they have just left.

Having their own queen, there are not so many bees leave that portion placed in another situation, and possessing the older brood the hive will soon be crowded, when the outside sheets of foundation are to be inserted one or two at a time in the centre of the brood nest. The number of frames to be allowed for breeding will depend upon the approach or return of the honey-flow, and it may even be necessary to remove some of the least filled with brood, where comb-honey is to be worked for, crowding the bees on to eight or nine of the combs most densely packed with brood. I formerly practised

## Contraction

both in summer and winter, but with the institution of my non-swarming system it is found unnecessary either for summer or winter. When increasing, however, it is the only way to make the most of the honey harvest, by thus curtailing the powers of the queen in less populous colonies. Treatment for either comb or extracted honey with divided stocks will be as before mentioned ; but where

## Natural Increase

is permitted, the plan of proceeding will be somewhat different. Constant care and attention is needed where swarming is allowed, and if due precautions are not taken the prospects of a good harvest are ruined. In the first place we will consider my own method of

## Swarming without Increase.

Where a swarm is not seen to issue, a glance around at the entrances of the hives only should show the bee-keeper from which it came. Hitherto, all was life and activity, but look ! here 'is your hive with the entrance clear of bees, and but a few returning, while hardly one is seen to issue ; it is the " calm after a storm.". A closer inspection of the hive will reveal the true state of affairs, and now remove all but one or two of the combs to another hive standing by the original, with the entrance turned away from the same. Secure the swarm in a skep or any other convenient article, standing the same upon the ground with clear space for ventilation under, and shade above. As soon as most of the bees have entered or clustered about the skep, carry the same to their original location and shake them into the hive, having previously arranged six or seven frames with full sheets of foundation, or ½-inch strips of such ; and not more than two frames of brood near the centre, with dummies at either side.

The sections are to be replaced on the new swarm which will soon receive so many bees in addition from the removed combs that the remaining population will give up any idea of again swarming, and will destroy all but one queen. When the latter is mated and laying, the brood will be hatched, when the old queen left with the swarm is to be destroyed, and on the following evening unite the two lots with the young queen presiding. The united stock should not have more than ten or eleven frames in all, while the remainder of the broodless combs can be used for extracting purposes.

Where more than one young queen may be desired, break up the removed combs into the necessary number of nuclei with a queen cell to each on the eighth day after swarming, and re-unite as soon as the queens can be appropriated.

For obtaining one swarm from each stock, and in desiring to

## Prevent After-swarms,

proceed in the same way, except that the removed combs and bees are to be placed at a distance from the old position, and no uniting takes place. This plan of obtaining one swarm and throwing the whole working force with the same, while making it a certainty that the other portion will cause no. further trouble was well known to, and practised by, most of the old masters. In this case, there is no time wasted in cutting out queen cells, an operation that cannot be tolerated in a modern honey-producing apiary. Should there be any fear of the bees being strong enough to swarm again, a few more shaken off with the new swarm will settle that matter. As soon as the young queen, or one already on hand, has six or seven combs crowded with brood, supers may be placed on her hive also, at the same time giving two more empty combs or foundation near the centre. Upon removal of the sections there will probably be hardly an ounce of honey in the stock combs, when another empty comb or two must be inserted and feeding be followed up, so that the brood nest is gradually reduced and the combs stored for winter.

## Securing a Profit in Poor Seasons

is a matter of the greatest moment, but one seldom successfully grappled with by any beekeeper. The hives are arranged for the summer's work, and should the weather continue unfavourable for the storing of honey the owner sees the season gradually slipping away from him while he remains perfectly helpless. He does, perhaps, feed when necessary, and return swarms as they may issue, but this is too frequently the full extent of his 'management' (?), while the end of the season finds him only out of pocket on the year's unsatisfactory work.

Even if only an improvement in the quality of the stock had been made during the year, there could have been no loss, but, on the other hand, a decided gain. Indeed, it is the first duty of the progressive apiarist to rear young queens yearly from his best stocks, or by purchasing desirable queens from apiaries that can be relied upon for excellence and healthiness of stock.

However bad it may seem, there is almost certain to be one or two fair weather spells of a few days' duration, when, by a careful amalgamation of forces, fairly good returns may be secured ; and, even in uncertain weather, stocks in good heart, placed close to any heavy crop, are almost sure to do well, and repay any trouble taken in removing them.

Where there is a demand for it, increase should be obtained as soon as it is found the season is likely to end with no surplus honey. Besides improving his stock and disposing of surplus colonies, there are other plans that may be followed to prevent loss during a season considered unfavorable for honey.

The cultivation of fruit will be a great advantage, and pay both ways if close at home ; and where it is convenient to grow large flowering field crops, with due thought for the bees as well as the profit on the hay or seeds, a failure in the honey returns will seldom be known.

CHAPTER XVIII.

# FEEDING AND FEEDERS.

WHEN and how to feed are questions of considerable importance to bee-keepers generally. In the apiary where bees and queens are raised for sale, feeding has often to be resorted to, as nothing is so exhaustive as the production of bees and queens on a large scale. Many colonies are reduced to such an extent that the remaining bees are occupied entirely in brood rearing, forced on to the utmost by the master. Honey is quite a secondary object; bees *must* be had. Consequently, honey cannot always be obtained even when the average colony is storing, and the forcing process must therefore be kept up by some substitute.

## Dry Sugar Feeding.

For spring feeding generally, and for use with nuclei, I have found nothing so stimulative as my plan of dry sugar feeding. The feeder consists of a hollow dummy with one side hinged on simple wire nails and held by the same above; or by staples turned at right angles to project over the margin below and a turned wire inserted at either corner at the top, which can be moved out of the way to allow of easily removing the side. The space between the sides should not be more than one inch, or comb will frequently be built therein.

Sugar known as Porto Rico, a soft, moist article, is used, being pressed in tightly, and the bees, entering above the movable side, which does not reach the top bar by $\frac{1}{4}$-inch, are soon busily engaged in reducing the food to syrup.

In spring it is necessary that the moisture of the hive be retained by placing American oilcloth next above the frames and plenty of warm material above that. All that is required is that the air does not become too dry, and then the sugar will attract moisture to itself and greatly aid the bees in their own processes of adding the necessary liquids. If so little covering is placed above the non-porous cloth that condensation takes place, the sugar is used up too rapidly and the queen crowded out ; especially a's the temperature is reduced enough that the brood nest cannot be extended.

The feeders (Fig. 11) are placed as an ordinary frame at the outside of the brood nest and the bees allowed only so many combs that they are crowded into them.

Another very serviceable frame feeder I have in use holds 9 or 10 lbs,, and is 3 inches across inside, The bottom is simply a sheet of finely perforated tin placed in an arched form, so that the bees may cluster under and appropriate the sugar through the perforations.

## Syrup Feeders

used in my own apiaries dispense with the tedious process of preparation by cooking as hitherto carried out.

If a stock happens to be very short of stores in spring, I find it best to give a feed of syrup to put the bees in good heart, and then follow with the dry sugar. In autumn, when surplus receptacles are removed, it may be too early to finish off feeding all at once, and it is well to give ten or fifteen pounds of syrup immediately and finish gradually with a ten-pound dry feeder. This is, of course, where all the honey has been placed above, but where any have considerable stores on hand but not enough to winter, the balance must be made up rapidly with syrup not later than the end of September.

## Simmins' Syrup Frame Feeder

(Fig. 53) holds about twelve pounds ; is $4\frac{1}{2}$ inches wide, and otherwise of the " standard " frame dimensions. The joints are all tongued and well put together that no leakage may occur, though it is advisable to paint the whole inside to prevent saturation. There is a slot along the top on one side nearest the bees, by which they are allowed to enter a ¾-inch passage between the outer and inner wall, where a good footing is obtained while taking up the syrup. The sugar is held clear of the bottom by a piece of perforated tin in an arched form, thus admitting of a free circulation of liquids under the dissolving sugar. No cooking therefore is necessary, as the usual quantity of sugar and water (a pound of sugar to half a pint of water) soon amalgamate in the form of syrup. The proportions named happen to be correct for this system, as it will be found that a residue of sugar will be given where more than the pound is placed in the half pint of water. Another feeder for the top of the hive is the

### Circular "Amateur,"

which I have arranged upon the same principle, as will be readily understood by the illustration (Fig. 50). This holds about 7 or 8 lbs. at a time, and the inner funnel leading up to the syrup passage around the same is lined with wood, or a lamp-wick can be used leading down into the cluster in cool weather ; though if feeding is necessary at such times it is always more satisfactory if the syrup is warmed. Among

### Bottle-feeders,

we have the "Raynor" (Fig. 51) arranged to give a graduated supply, with a projecting point attached to the perforated metal cap of the bottle, indicating by the figures to which it points on the stand the number of holes to which the bees have access. The underside of the excavated block is lined with warm material, though generally of the kind that is annoying to the bees, and which they soon tear away. If painted with wax it would be equally as warm, and more appreciated by the bees.

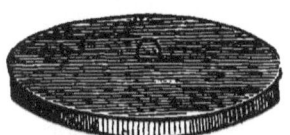
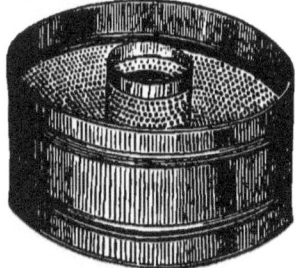
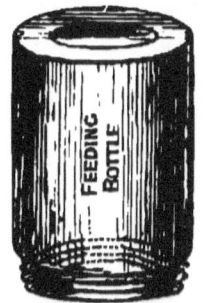

Fig. 50.
Circular "Amateur" Feeder.

SECTION OF STAND
51.
Raynor Bottle Feeder.

Fig. 52.
Self-acting Syrup Can.

N

Messrs. Abbott have long had something similar, though more simple and less expensive ; but there is one great disadvantage with all bottle-feeders, in that they are subject to atmospheric pressure, and with a sudden rise of temperature the expansion causes much waste of syrup. The syrup has usually been boiled when prepared for this class of feeder, but for my own use I have large cylinders on the self-acting feeder principle which reduce about 2 cwt. of loaf sugar at a time, the syrup being drawn off by a treacle valve at the bottom. The syrup-can illustrated (Fig. 52) will also be found very suitable for smaller quantities, saving much time and trouble in cooking : the self-acting principle being the great feature in this, as in my Champion Feeders.

A very simple feeder is one adopted by myself some years since when using frames 16 inches by 10 inches. Good sound wood is selected, and plain boards fastened on each side of a frame of any desired width. Put the nails in rather close together and paint all joints with white lead before making up. The top bar is ¾-inch thick with projections reduced to ⅜-inch. This is secured by four screws so that it can be removed for cleaning. The syrup is poured in at the circular hole, after turning back the quilt, and the bees go in by a slot on the side ; no float is needed ; Fig. 54.

In many apiaries feeding is seldom resorted to, but there are times of dearth when valuable colonies would be utterly ruined were it not for the timely assistance rendered by the owner—assistance that sooner or later is repaid a hundredfold.

Of course, if feeding is absolutely necessary after the surplus receptacles have once been occupied, it must be simply from ".hand to mouth," that nothing be stored in supers; while it may even be desirable to remove such entirely, replacing them when better times put in an appearance.

### Feeding without Feeders

is something that needs our attention before closing this chapter. Of the various methods offered for filling stock

combs with syrup, to be placed in the centre of the brood
nest for stimulation, or near the outside for storing, no plan
can be so effective and simple as that employed by Mr. W.
Raitt, of Scotland. He used a common syringe, placing the
comb in a drip pan, while driving the syrup into the cells.
The filled combs are carried to the hives requiring them,
while sometimes a chamber is filled up with them and placed
bodily under the stock chamber which has to be stored.

A simple method of giving " dry sugar " is that of first
placing a layer of strainer cloth upon the frames; the sugar
above that, and pressed into a compact mass, with the usual
quilting next that, nicely tucked up to keep all warm. Common paper will do in place of the straining cloth if two or three
holes are first made through to give the bees a start.

### Feeding with Candy

is another matter requiring serious consideration, for certainly
it is a process more frequently abused than properly used.
This article has generally been brought into requisition where
stocks from any cause have run short of food too late in the
Autumn, or during Winter, when it is supposed other plans
of feeding could not be adopted. But with due care, no stock
need be left alone long enough to get into that state.

It should be distinctly understood that

### No Feeding should take place in Winter,

and though candy is often recommended, it is far better to
unite to a well-stored stock in the autumn than to feed in any
way during the months of repose. If a stock is found deficient
in stores at the latter part of winter, then give combs of sealed
food with as little disturbance as possible; placing such flat
on top of the frames and covering up warm if the weather is
very bad. It is better at any time in Winter to give a dose
of hot thick syrup, if only two or three pounds, than to rely

on candy. The object is to get the bees along until February is well advanced, and to feed not at all until then if possible.

No stock, however disheartened, will refuse to take a bottle of hot syrup, placed directly over the cluster on to the naked frames, and in two days or less they have the best of food around them, with but little excitement, while candy is a cause of constant activity. When bees begin to move, then that article can be used to advantage, and may even be used in place of any other feeding up to the approach of the honey season. For

## Making Candy.

the usual proportions recommended are one pint of water and one wine glass of vinegar to eight pounds of good loaf sugar. This is stirred well over a clear fire until all is melted, and is then allowed to simmer with occasional stirring, until a drop or two placed on a cold plate will almost immediately set hard, or will at least not stick to the plate. A large news sheet placed on a table with the edges folded and turned up at right angles all round, and these blocked upright with pieces of wood or other articles, will form the most convenient receptacle for general use. As soon as the surface is set, it should be cut across with a knife so that suitable sized cakes may be had without waste in breaking.

Where systematic Candy feeding is to be carried on in Spring, the better plan is to pour the hot liquid into wired frames, fastening them down to the table or a flat board, with paper between, by means of a couple of nails, or specially prepared blocks.

The vinegar can be dispensed with and a much better quality of Candy secured by using only one pint of water with one pound of honey to eight pounds of sugar.

## Out-Door Feeding.

I must not fail to notice this question as it is one of con-siderable importance, and yet just here is a rock on which all hopes of success may often be dashed to pieces. It is at once the most desirable method of feeding, and the greatest of stimulants to increased energy and development on the part of the bees ; while it can also be shewn as the most destructive to bee-life where all the points to be considered are not well understood.

## During the Spring

nothing of the kind should be allowed until the population of the hives has been largely *renewed* by young bees, and then with due care in placing the feeding apparatus in a warm sheltered corner, the results will be remarkable.

At least double the usual quantity of water must be added to the syrup and the feeders placed some distance from the apiary, that robbing may not be induced.

## In the Autumn

out-door feeding should not be carried on later than September, and if the supply can be kept warm all the time, it will be a decided advantage. No more bees will then be lost than are old and that will be quite useless, and in any case would hardly live to help winter their colony, while the stores are arranged in the best possible position, and sufficient young bees are brought into existence to place the hives in good condition for Winter.

It is some twelve years since I first practised this kind of feeding, and having tried nearly every way that could be thought of, I have found the

## Most suitable Feeders for the purpose

to be large glass or other jars, with porous cloths tied over the mouths, and inverted. Any number of these can be used, turning them down over boards with circular openings cut out, that they may be held in a suspended position. Float feeders and other similar arrangements are sure to go wrong, causing many deaths, but with the above, all is clean, there can be no daubing, and empty jars can soon be replaced by others, or the whole quickly cleared away should any cause arise for so doing.

### Feeding by Syrup-filled Combs in Spring

is another process which requires a degree of caution in carrying out, such as few are aware of. The excitement caused by introducing whole combs of unsealed food before a younger element of life has been created, causes unnecessary flights with its consequently increased death rate among the older inhabitants of the hives. The stimulation is apparent, but the anticipated increase of a youthful addition to the population is not forthcoming; for though almost at the birth, frequently the sadly wanted natural fostering warmth has been rendered non-existant by a too hasty attempt at stimulation.

## CHAPTER XIX

# BUYING, PACKING, AND MOVING BEES.

I N an early chapter, much has already been explained as to the best time to buy bees. If possible, they should be obtained in hives that are in general use, and can be adapted to modern management.

In most cases the seller packs the bees and delivers them to the rail, the buyer paying carriage ; but if he has the time and can make it convenient, the buyer will find it greatly to his advantage to see them packed and delivered to the railway company, especially where many hives are concerned.

Though some are more suited to the purpose than others, I have yet to see the hive, legs or no legs, that could not be turned " top-side-down " for travelling ; and all should be so sent as the combs then ride more securely, having their base resting upon the top bar of the inverted frame. Tapes may or may not be fastened round the frames to enclose the combs more securely ; but to dispense with this, where I can make my own selection, I use combs that are well fastened down the side bars of the frame.

Shade must be provided in hot weather, with more ventilation than at other times. Bees are lost more from want of ventilation in travelling than anything else, and due provision should be made according to the number of the occupants in

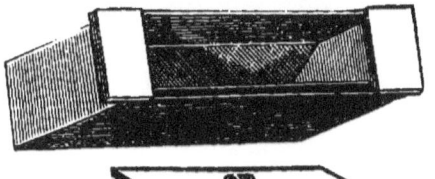

Fig. 53.
Champion Frame Syrup Feeder.

Fig. 54.
Simplicity Frame
Feeder.

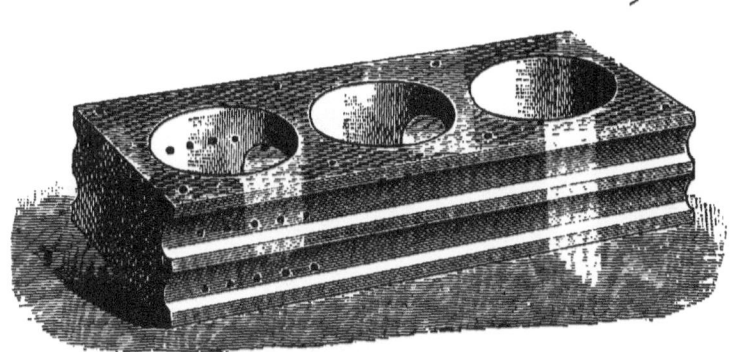

Fig. 55.
Benton Queen Postal Cage.

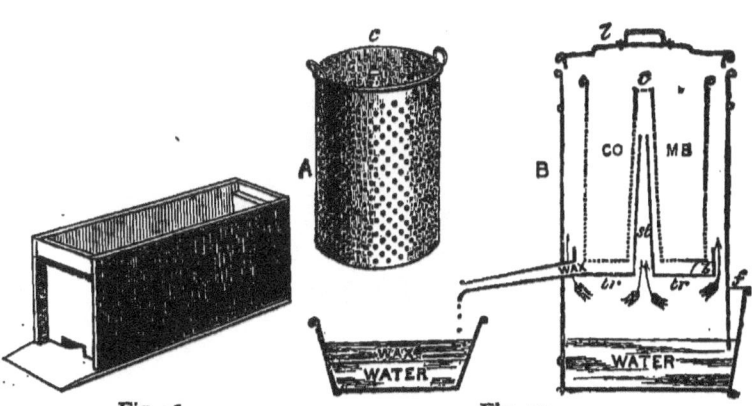

Fig 56.
Nucleus Hive.

Fig. 57.
Sectional View of Wax Extractor.

whatever receptacle may be provided. If sacking can be arranged to give shade and at the same time exclude light without interfering with the admission of air, bees will travel and stand confinement very much better than where they are continually striving to get out, and thus to a great extent impeding free circulation.

## Packing Stocks.

Before inverting the hive, fasten a thin board along the whole length of the hive at the ends of the frames, overlapping these at least one inch. A piece of porous sacking is first to be placed above the frames and held in position by a few tacks till the slips of wood are fixed. With the left hand find where the frame ends come, and with a bradawl bore a hole through the thin board into each bar ; then insert French nails *pressed* not quite home. Screws are to be used with this exception, as little hammering should be allowed for fear of injuring the comb attachments.

We have to provide for a free circulation of air under, after the hive is inverted ; therefore on each upper side, parallel with the frames, thick strips of wood are to be screwed, so that these only will rest on the ground when turned over. The entrance may be closed with perforated zinc before or after, as is most convenient. The packing can take place several days before moving, if desired, leaving only the entrance to be closed on the eve of departure. In very hot weather for long journeys additional ventilation should be provided by holes bored at the sides and covered inside with perforated material, or an additional storey or half-storey can be given under the other before inversion.

By inverting the combs we not only place their weight upon, instead of depending from their base, but also provide that there is free circulation throughout the hive above them ; whereas in the natural position the heated air ascending is unable to escape and tends still further to weaken the foundation of the combs.

## When delivered on Rail,

or placed in vans, the combs should always travel in a line parallel with the road, so that with any incline, or sudden movement, they are not thrown to one side. When necessary. to tier up the hives, place boards between each set. Plenty of straw is needed to give them an easy motion, but on no account is it to be arranged so that the inverted hives rest directly upon it, though some must be packed between to prevent sliding, or jolting against each other. Place a good layer first upon the floor, spread it out evenly, and then lay boards down; on these place the first set of hives; then straw and boards again, thus always keeping a clear space under the sacking next the frames.

All covers and odd material must be packed separately, and where the stock hives are simple square boxes, with no projection whatever, the entire process will be more satisfactory and expeditious.

## For Export,

additional care will be necessary, while a sponge must be provided at one side in a perforated box, with directions requesting that the same may be moistened occasionally; or a zinc vessel may be supplied with a cotton wick held in a funnel reaching nearly to the bottom that the water cannot be spilled.

It may be necessary, according to the strength of the colony, to give an outer case, thoroughly ventilated to provide for excessive heat; though when it is known that bees have to undergo a high temperature, a nucleus only will travel far better and give more satisfactory results than a full colony.

## On receipt of the Bees,

they should be placed out where they are to stand permanently. The packing need not be removed for a day or so, but the entrances are to he opened as soon as the bees are a little quiet. Do not liberate each hive in rotation, but go from one spot to another as far distant as possible, and so let the first quiet down before a neighbouring hive is opened.

It is well not to examine the interior of the hives for two or three days, that the bees may have first noted their location; but it will then be necessary to determine if any queens have been lost, which frequently is the case. Where any are gone it will be desirable to unite to others at once if this happens to be the first stock of the apiarist; but when other colonies are on hand one may be able to insert another rather than unite.

## Packing Queens.

An admixture of honey and sugar, first mentioned in Rev. L. L. Langstroth's book as a substitute for honey in wintering, was afterwards used by Mr. I. R. Good, another American, in queen cages when transmitted by the post. However, perfection had yet to come ; the food was right, the candy was "good," but until the introduction of F. Benton's mailing cage, general success was not attained. Queens may now be sent by post just as safely as an ordinary letter, and Benton's cage has rendered the system absolutely perfect, though until recently through some short-sightedness, or prejudice on the part of the postal authorities, many foreign queens have been returned to the senders.

## The Benton Cage

consists of three compartments; one is ventilated for general accommodation, and particularly for advantage to the bees under high temperatures ; from this a small passage communicates with the central compartment, otherwise having no ventilation. The last has another small opening leading into the third space wherein is

## The Food.

which is made by thoroughly incorporating with finely powdered loaf sugar just sufficient liquid honey to form a thick

paste ; this should be almost dry, and give no sign of
"running " under any temperature.

It is best made up some time before actually required for
use, so that any excess of moisture may descend, leaving the
upper portion just right for the cages.  When the compartment
is filled a sheet of wax or a piece of parchment covers the
opening, while a thin lid of wood fits over the whole, being
secured with brads or tacks.  (See Fig. 55.)

## Inserting the Bees.

The lid is first to be tacked on only at one corner, at the
side of the food compartment.  Hold the cage in the left hand
with the thumb on the lid just above the ventilated chamber,
and now pick from the combs about a dozen young bees with
the right hand, inserting them one at a time while the thumb
moves the lid back to receive each in its turn.  The queen is
to be put in last to make sure of no mistake, when the
remainder of the tacks can be driven in.

If the weather is cold more bees must accompany the
queen, and additional warmth may be given by outside packing,
though this is seldom necessary with Benton's cage.  Instead
of the brad holes I have found a sawcut through the end more
effective for ventilating in hot weather.

## Packing Swarms.

A "rough-and-ready" way is to tie a piece of strainer cloth
over the mouth of a skep in which the swarm may have been
taken ; but for long distances something more substantial is
necessary, and a frame of honey will be required.

The box must be as light as is possible consistent with
strength, and ventilation must be given on at least two
opposite sides.  I have had very good results with air space
all round the top, the lid being raised and secured to the main
body with perforated zinc.

Swarms should always be purchased by weight, and the buyer ought to insist upon receiving no other. There are 3,500 bees to the pound, and four or five pounds would give a good working swarm. The plan of offering swarms containing so many thousand bees, when in reality not more than a third of the number make up the swarm forwarded, is becoming a thing of the past, and I do not suppose many would be caught in the trap now; nevertheless, swarms of no guaranteed weight are still advertised, and it is time bee-keepers set their faces against the practice.

## Weighing Bees.

Where natural or other swarms are weighed after clustering inside the travelling box, they can be first secured and carried to the scales, and the weight marked upon the label. If they have to go a long journey, either place a feeding bottle over the zinc until starting or see that a frame with sufficient sealed stores is securely fixed in before the swarm is hived; the weight of such comb and the box to be noted, and presently deducted from the gross weight.

Where a definite quantity is ordered, the scales are to be carried to the hive by any convenient arrangement that provides correct balance; take the weight of the package, and if the opening is not wide enough to admit a comb end-way, use a funnel lined with zinc. Now make sure of the queen and then shake from the combs the necessary quantity of bees, and insert the queen last of all; close at once and pack for the journey.

They are to be first smoked in the usual way, and all the time they do not miss the queen, the bulk of the bees shot into the box will remain simply clustering on the sides. The operation should take place in early morning or towards evening as the bees are more restful, and they can be put up in less time as there are more at home. Give food if necessary as before.

I consider the most satisfactory way and the more profit-able to the purchaser when wishing to establish a stock of any new variety is to get them in

## Three-frame Nuclei ;

but I do not mean such as are often sent out, and as some I have myself received from abroad with- not enough bees to cover one of the frames; but such as can be built up with little trouble by the receiver.

To make up a fair nucleus of three frames, take from a strong hive all the bees from one comb, and one comb full of brood where young bees are rapidly coming forth, with all the bees thereon.  Place the brood comb at the centre of the small hive, the other bees having first been shaken in, and look up a comb partly stored to place on each side.  Screw the lid down after inserting the queen ; place wire nails through into the frames at each end, and invert as for full stocks.  Strong combs should be selected, and sufficient ventilation given without danger of chilling the brood.

The frame of hatching brood will presently give enough bees to cover three combs, so that with the other bees a queen gets a good start, though if the apiarist has them to spare, another comb of brood in like condition added every seven days will do wonders in building up a full colony.

## Standard Colonies

of definite quantities are now offered for sale, and are far more reliable than stocks bought in the old 'hap-hazard' kind of way.  For so many combs offered, one may rely upon having that number covered with bees, and all except the two outer combs pretty well filled with brood.  Thus a six-frame stock should have four frames of brood, an eight-frame six of brood, and so on.

## CHAPTER XX.

# HOUSE APIARIES, STORE ROOMS, &c.

I T would be a difficult matter to give hard and fast rules for putting up buildings to suit every bee-keeper who owns a. large number of colonies. One may have premises that with little or no alteration suit his requirements. Another may. have no room to put up convenient sheds, or the situation is such that any given plan could not be carried out.

I will therefore give ground plans of buildings, &c., that I have found to be convenient, and the reader may then make such modifications as may suit his own particular requirements, having the general idea in mind.

### The Building

as Fig. 58 is put up with 3-inch by 2-inch scantling as the framework, and ¾-inch by 6-inch boards, matched and beaded. The roof leans to a stone wall at the back, and is there 10 feet from the ground. The front of the main shed is 6 feet from ground to roof; the outer store about 4 feet at the front.

### The Workshop

is 20 feet by 12 feet, with communication to the apiary at **D**, passing a shallow water tank which is constantly supplied, and has cork dust floating on top for the bees to settle upon.

o

This article, recommended by a correspondent in the *British Bee Journal*, is more satisfactory than anything I have tried for the purpose. Only the coarser material is used, after the fine dust is sifted from it.

The plan, to a great extent, explains itself; F R are frame-racks for hanging up frames as put together, or foundation when inserted ready for use. C C are closed comb-cupboards, with ventilation through the hinged doors at both top and bottom by auger holes covered with perforated zinc.

The bench stands in front of

## The Window,

the panes of which are in one piece, and *do not reach the bottom of the frame* by ½-inch ; thus, when combs are first taken into the workroom any stray bees soon find their way out, as also at any time. To prevent them returning, perforated zinc is tacked outside along the bottom of the frame, and reaching 6 or 7 inches above the said opening, with a space of ⅜-ths of an inch between it and the glass. The above arrangement with fixed windows I prefer to any revolving sash, because a room may be left for days together, and the bee-keeper knows that not a bee will lose its life in the vain endeavour to escape, as with the other which needs constant attention to prevent much loss.

From the workshop we pass into the

## Honey Room,

where by the passage from end to end the recess is occupied by frame-racks which will accommodate several thousand frames, empty combs, or those stored brought in from the apiary for extracting. At the other side of the passage we see the counter ;. with staging on two sides near that, where crates of both bottled and comb-honey can be stored.

The open space gives room for extracting, arranged with or without a stage to assist in drawing from the extractor, as the

apiarist may desire. Passing the other door, **D,** we again look upon a portion of the apiary, with the gateway **G** leading out of the premises. **O D** is an open doorway to the store for odd materials, timber, &c. The latter may be placed overhead in the workshop for greater convenience. **L W** is a latticed window, giving all the light required besides the open doorway. The honey room is lighted by a window in the roof, having no arrangement for clearing out bees as this is done in the workrooms before our honey is taken in, and every care is taken to keep out any intruder, while at the same time a thorough change of air is provided.

The floor of the honey room must be concreted, but the other is not of so much importance. It is sometimes recommended that a paraffin stove be kept burning in the honey store, but with the skylight sufficiently large, the heat of the sun will be quite enough to complete the ripening process, taking care that it does not shine directly upon the honey.

## A COVERED APIARY,

as illustrated, for 150 colonies, occupies a space 118 feet by 50 feet, being compactly built, with the entrances arranged so that no two are alike within several yards. The base of all the walls is a plank, 6 inches by 3 inches, under which is laid a single row of 3-inch bricks as with the building first mentioned. All the framework is of 3-inch by 2-inch scantling and matched boards as before, put on when dry. The ground plan is as seen by Fig. 59. The only door communicating with the outside leads first into a closed room, 50 feet by 12 feet. Just beyond the centre we have the honey safe and extracting room, which stands two feet clear of the ground with woven wire on two sides opposite the window. Steps lead to the door, which is carefully fitted, and no bees are able to get in.

The long room has two windows also with the glass arranged that no bees are ever found dead inside, as before

mentioned.   Stray bees are here disposed of before the honey
goes into the safe.   Between the latter ʻand the outer door
stands a table, 12 feet by 3 feet, for general manipulations.
On either side with intervening passages are shelves for
storing crates and other materials.

The larger shed has a span roof, 10 feet high at the centre,
dropping to 8 feet at the sides, and upon turning to the right
after entering by the outer door, we can⁚pass into either of the
parallel bee sheds, each of which is 8 feet high, dropping to
5 feet on the lower wall.   The hives are situated all along
inside the south wall, with flight holes cut through, and the
outside of the same varied in appearance.   Here no glass is
used, but shutters provided at suitable intervals.

## The advantages

that can be claimed for a covered apiary are as follows :—The
bees as well as the master have shade during the heat of the
day at the season most attention is required.   Shelter is
afforded from wind and rain, so that any necessary work is
carried on without hindrance; and lastly the entire arrangement provides for a great saving of time in that all is compactly
arranged in the smallest convenient space.

Provision is made for 150 colonies, and nuclei can be placed
in narrow hives close to the walls about four feet from the
ground, resting on the central rail of the framework.

## Bee-houses so-called,

but being merely cupboards, with two or more rows of hives,
leaving neither room for tiering nor ordinary manipulations,
are not worthy a place in the modern apiary ; moreover, no
arrangement in larger houses can be in any sense convenient
where an attempt is made to arrange an upper and lower row
of standard hives.

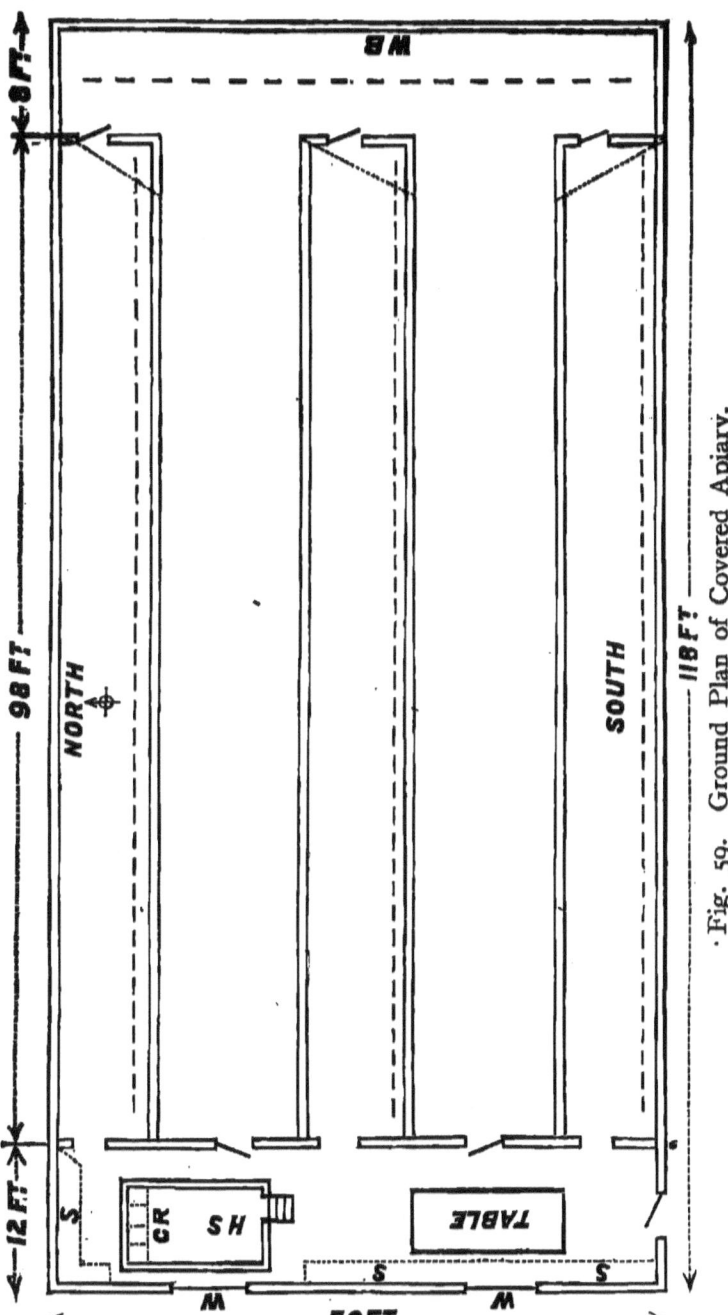

Fig. 59. Ground Plan of Covered Apiary.

W Windows. S Shelves or Staging. H S Honey Safe, Extracting Room, and Store Room. C R Comb Racks. — Position of Hives. W B Wind-Break,

CHAPTER XXI.

# THE PRODUCTION OF WAX;
## AND NON-USE OF FOUNDATION.

THE more one studies the matter the more is he convinced that wax should be a profitable product of the apiary. We have been told over and over again that the bees consume 20 lbs. of honey while producing 1 lb. of wax therefrom. Upon the face of it the idea is merely theoretical, as in the first place it is ridiculous to presume that an article costing, if we say only 5s. (20 lbs. of honey at 3d.) could be sold for 1s. 6d. Supply and demand regulate prices, and, as a matter of fact, wax is comparatively scarce ; therefore it is time the question of cost is set at rest once and for all.   In making

### A Test by Experiment,

there were several important factors to be considered ; the bees experimented with had access to both water and pollen, but no brood was allowed at the time.   The experiment was carried out where the bees were not confined to the hive, and they gathered no other food than that supplied to them for the purpose.   A test of this kind should be carried out under a high temperature, and a fair swarm used for the occasion, but in my own case I had to be content with rather a low temperature but the result was very satisfactory, and I found that 6½ lbs. of honey gave a pound of wax.

## Aids to Production.

The apiarist who has all the colonies and all the combs he requires is the one who will make the production of wax profitable. He will have a great deal from cappings in extracting, and many an odd piece, all of which should be placed in some convenient receptacle till enough is obtained to run down. There are the queen cells even; shavings from combs when reduced to brood thickness in spring; also the scrapings from the tops of frames, not including the propolis.

Then, again, new worker combs can be produced in spring between the others containing brood, while feeding dry sugar, at a great saving over foundation; the apiarist then being able to run down his more irregular combs, or those that are getting too old; or, as is sometimes the case, the wax being perished, such would only be torn down by the bees, as they do not appreciate combs that have been out of use for a whole season, and if possible all should be passed through the hive every year to keep them in good order.

During the season that bees are storing heavily I have reason to believe that the secretion of wax is continually going on, and if the scales cannot be utilised they are allowed to drop and be carried out as so much refuse. Now the space allowed below the brood chamber provides that full employ-ment shall ever be given should it happen from any cause that the supers are not removed in due time and the bees there kept busy. Thus we have another step towards the produc-tion of wax. When one desires

## To Produce Wax in Quantity,

a colony must be run for extracted honey, and at suitable intervals alternate the combs of brood or stores with starters only in the frames. Between the stored combs these would be built rather thin, but the sealed combs are to be removed and the honey extracted as soon as the new ones are built to about two-thirds of the frame capacity ; other empty frames take their place, and so on in rotation.  This process cannot be carried out to any extent between brood combs, except as described for spring work or when a young queen presides over the colony, otherwise some drone comb will be built ; and the production of useless drones shows a great defect in management.

Another plan, by which a large number of colonies can be kept and much wax produced at little expense of labour, is to place several chambers fitted up with starters under the brood nest early in May.  The bees will gradually work down, and the production of brood will be regulated in accordance with the amount of income, and no trouble with swarming will be experienced.

The most economical plan for producing even and useful worker combs is that of arranging small colonies of three and four combs with vigorous bees and queen.  Shift about occasionally, making nuclei on old stand to dispose of the older bees and so prevent the clogging of combs with honey.  Keep all closed up warm and feed gently, but always.  Put in a frame with narrow guide only, and in three or four days such colonies will produce a beautiful worker comb nearly filling the frame and being generally crowded with eggs.  These may be utilised as required, and the same process continued. ·For three months at a stretch such small (carefully-tended) colonies will continue the process, giving something like two dozen good combs, while the brood removed will represent two powerful stocks.  Such a profit, and saving of outlay in foundation, should satisfy the most economic bee keeper.

### Where Swarms have been Hived upon Starters,

I have avoided the building of drone combs by placing the frames rather less than $1\frac{3}{8}$-inch from centre to centre.  This point appears to have been overlooked by many in America who have followed Doolittle, who for a long time stood almost alone in his endeavour to show that foundation was used in many cases at a loss.

W. Z. Hutchinson took up Doolittle's idea, and has been the cause of the plan becoming more generally used : but not only does the complaint come that much drone comb is built, but also that

## Pollen is Stored in the Sections.

The latter trouble also I learned to avoid when hiving swarms upon full sheets of foundation in my endeavour to get the best work started in the sections. Just as I hived swarms upon foundation (when made by division), I now put them upon starters, with the addition of two combs of brood; one with uncapped larvæ, and the other having brood hatching. Thus the bees have room to store the pollen carried the first day or two, without spoiling the partly finished sections when they happen to be removed from the old stock to the swarm ; and what is of equal importance, there is just sufficient brood to make up for wear and tear before a general hatching would otherwise take place. Moreover the queen is kept below without the useless and expensive addition of the excluder zinc Mr. Hutchinson is obliged to use where starters only are given under the sections.

My plan is not to throw the bees entirely into the sections as soon as they are hived, but simply to prevent the production of an excess of brood in the height of the season, and with the two combs of brood so arranged the colony is worth wintering after the season is over ; whereas in the other case several have to be united to get a fair stock. But, I am told, the bees will not work in the sections with so much room below! Have I not already shown how full stocks will do so with plenty of room under or in front of the stock combs ? And if your bees will not go into the supers, when they are strong enough and honey is to be had, do not wait for their pleasure, but *put them in* by either of two ways.

## To make the Bees go into the Sections,

first secure the queen and cage her above the sections for a few hours, and when you go to the hive you will find the super crowded; remove her quietly and let her go in by the entrance. Another plan I have found successful is to place the crate on a sheet of paper on the ground, raised on one side that the bees may draw under, when many of the bees are to be shaken off the frames close to the same when they will cluster in the sections. They may be thrown on top without lifting the crate, and though some will of course return when the super is replaced, our object is accomplished.

This is best done towards evening, and when desirable to add other swarms within a few days, these can be hived in upper crates without their queen.

All the above has reference to the profitable production of wax, and I shall be excused for bringing these particulars of management in here, more particularly as the whole question has received but little attention from bee-keepers generally.

## When Foundation may be used to advantage.

Now I do not consider that foundation is always used in the stock chamber at a loss; in fact it can be adopted at considerable profit when extension of stock is the object.

A bee-keeper may have to increase his stock of both bees and combs, and then considerable time will be gained by taking advantage of foundation; though it should be borne in mind that increase is obtained at the expense of honey.

When the honey season arrives we have to be prepared with plenty of storage room, and therefore nothing less than full sheets of foundation can be tolerated in our sections, while if already drawn out in preparation for the harvest, the results will be far better. If suitable foundation with a thin base is used there will be no difference to be distinguished between such combs and those built from starters only, while the appearance of the surface when capped will be much better than that of those so often finished off with drone cells.

' While the profitable production of wax will be carried out by those who have completed their stock, much will depend upon locality, as well as the culture of bees most suited to the purpose.

## Wax Extractors.

Solar wax extractors are frequently used, with a large surface of glass, on a frame; all being air-tight enclosing a perforated vessel to take the wax and a pan under, but these are not so satisfactory as those worked by steam. A cross section of a suitable wax refiner is shown in two sections. A piece of fine flannel should be stretched across, under the perforated comb holder A, thus thoroughly refining at the first operation. The wax running on to the false bottom passes out by the spout into a convenient receptacle. When it is required to work from a steam boiler, the steam pipe should enter just above the water line shown, and no water will be required below, as when placed over a stove. The wax will be of still finer quality if the vessel it runs into contains warm water.

The illustration is that of Mr. Cheshire's pattern, and is manufactured by Mr. Meadows, of Syston. (See Fig. 57).

## Cost of Producing Wax.

My experiment was conducted in a large flight room, 50 feet by 10 feet. A swarm of nearly 3 lbs. weight was made up and given frames, with a line of wax as a starter to each. I determined to avoid the complication that would arise if brood were produced, but at the same time it was necessary to have a fertile queen presiding, or the bees would not work to the best advantage. The new combs were therefore removed every three days, and though occasionally eggs were to be seen, no food was consumed in their production other than that fed to the queen. The removed combs were placed behind the division board, and were emptied of their contents by the bees, to be again used in filling fresh frames.

Thus without extracting, the combs were taken away perfectly dry, with the exception of the three last built; and to make sure of wasting none of this remaining honey the combs containing it were run down in a vessel with no added water. The bees had access to both pollen and water while building, and from 6 lbs. of honey fed to them they gave 6¼ ozs. of clear wax, with a balance of 15 ozs. of honey left over. ˙If I say an even pound left I shall be nearer the mark, as the bees had the means of loading themselves much more heavily than when the swarm was made, as they were then forced to consume what they had before commencing to build. Five pounds therefore giving that quantity of wax, it would be supposed that it takes 12⅔ lbs. of honey to give a pound. But our experiment is not yet completed ; the bees had to live during the twenty days taken to carry it out. Being in a con-fined area during autumn when the weather was far from being as warm as could be desired, the expense of production would be very much more than when new combs are built in the height of the season. The bees did not get on so fast, especially as the best combs were removed in time to prevent the produc-tion of brood, and towards the last the supply of honey became very limited.

## To Get at the Cost of Living,

after removing the last of the combs and balance of the honey, the bees were given just 1 lb. of honey in a feeder arranged so that they would not get it fast enough to go on building. After the fourth day there were 6 ozs. left ; but here is a little difficulty: they could not require 10 ozs. in that time, and on removing the feeder with balance of honey, and giving four empty combs they put about 2 ozs. into the cells. This would still leave 8 ozs. consumed, or 2 ozs. per day while in active flight. Then for the twenty days we have 40 ozs. consumed

to preserve life, which deducted from the 5 lbs. leaves 2 lbs..
8 ozs. actually used in producing the 6¼ ozs. of wax ; thus, to
produce 1 lb. of wax 6⅘ lbs. of honey would be consumed.

When the cost of living was carried out the bees were
reduced about one-third, so that 2 ozs. per day should be
within the mark. In the height of the season with everything
favourable it is only reasonable to say that the cost of production is really much less, and probably less than 5 lbs. of
honey are consumed in actually producing one pound of wax.

## Comparative Cost.     •

In the course of the experiment I found that about eight
standard frames (14 inches by 8½ inches) of new comb will
give one pound of refined wax. It is surprising what a large
amount of refuse is left after melting the most beautifully
white combs, so that the actual weight of wax obtained is
much less that that of the original combs. *Observe this* : one
pound of wax, costing the producer less than 1s. 6d., fills eight
frames with finished comb. To do this with foundation 1⅛ lb.
of that article is required, costing in hard cash at the least
2s. 6d. for the base only ; to this the bees add considerable of
their own production before the combs can be completed ;
making the total cost much over 3s. Facts are stubborn
things, and cannot be ignored.

CHAPTER XXII.

# MANAGEMENT FOR HEATHER HONEY.

HAVING had considerable experience in former years, between 1870 and 1880, in sending my bees every autumn to extensive heath-lands, the information placed before my readers in this chapter will doubtless prove of considerable value. Hitherto no work has given special treatment for the production of heather honey; and yet it is a subject of the first importance to hundreds of bee-keepers, nearly all of whom wish for some better method than they have had for making the most of this late harvest.

Late in the season bees must be close to, or in the midst of, the crop they are to gather from, and in the case of heather large quantities of honey can be, and often are, secured ; but in very many cases the stock combs receive, and are totally blocked up with, what the apiarist desires to get stored in the sections.

Heather honey being so thick, it is quite impossible to extract it unless removed as fast as gathered, and this is not desirable. It is usual for bees to crowd the stock combs late in the season, as many find to their cost ; but why is it so? It is not that the nights are cooler, as frequently the temperature at night is much higher in August than during May, when

P

bees work well in the supers. It is not even that the bees are aware that the season is drawing to a close, as many consider; but if we would go to the very starting point of the trouble, we shall find that

## The whole question centres upon the Queen,

as every bee-keeper may prove for himself, and as he will admit as he follows my statements.

Now, what is the condition of the colony which goes first into the supers in early summer? Have I not already shewn that the hive must be full of bees, and have every stock comb *literally crammed* with brood, when the honey *must* go into the sections? Well, go and do likewise for your heather crop! Imagine that you have another year, a new season coming in, instead of a late season in the same year; and then you will have your honey where you want it.

But, you say the bees will *not* breed to any extent late in the year. True, the same queen that you have used all the summer will be of no use to you in this emergency, and just here is the point. You are, then, to

## Use a Young Queen,*

and the best way to have one in readiness for every hive is to follow my plan of using every tenth colony for nuclei as already shewn. Your first harvest closes towards the latter part of July, and as soon as the supers can be removed, dethrone the old queen and unite the stock and nucleus. You now have a stronger colony and a young queen who will take good care that her domains are not crowded with honey. *Her* first season is just coming and the bees will act accordingly.

This is a special case and special treatment is required, as the honey nearly always comes in so freely that, by the old method, the already exhausted queens are soon crowded out

---

* See also Simmins' Non-Swarming Pamphlet (Feb., 1886).

and by the time the harvest is over, the workers are worn out; whereas with the young queen we have a good stock left, with bees still hatching to make up for the tremendous loss of life. More honey is accumulated because the population is larger and does not decrease as only too frequently has been the case.

Of course only worked-out combs are to be used in the sections, including those not completed from the first harvest, after being cleared by the extractor.

At the termination of the earlier harvest if any stores are left in the stock combs, the same should be extracted and, in

## Uniting with the Nucleus,

only those combs most crowded with brood should be used. The odd combs of brood can be given to one or more lots left at home. Some reader may say that his hives *are* crowded when his bees go to the moors. They may be, but like the queen such bees are already exhausted by their previous labours, and new blood is required throughout if one wishes to make the most of this last important harvest.

If necessary feed "from hand to mouth" after uniting, until time for the heather, but on no account feed heavily, as advised recently by a correspondent in the *British Bee Journal,* who hoped thereby to fill up the space the old queen could not occupy, expecting that the heather honey would all go above, and that when the bees came home they would require no more feeding. True indeed, for there would in many cases be no bees to require it. How utterly inconsistent, to add wear and tear, when the whole energy of our workers should be reserved for the storage of this last crop! And how very injudicious to crowd the queen out at the very time we require one that will still-further extend the brood nest in preparation for the good time near at hand.

' Moreover, it is a fact that no amount of false reasoning can gainsay, that where heavy feeding is done just before supering, especially in Spring, the *greater portion* of the syrup

thus fed *is stored above after the sections are put on*.   Thus the
result is both delusive and dishonest.

On the other hand, the process is so much like killing the
goose to get the golden egg, that one should bear in mind the
fact that heavy feeding causes the destruction of brood which
the bees do not hesitate to remove for the accommodation of
stores thus forced upon them, so that not .only does the bee-
keeper add wear. and tear without cause, but actually gets rid
of many young bees which should have been relied upon for
his heather harvest.   A young queen, the union of forces, and
*gentle stimulative feeding*, are just as necessary now as when
preparing for the first honey flow of the season.

### When Moving to the Heather,

everything should be got ready and loaded on the vans over-
night, and if not desirable to travel during the night the journey
ought not to be delayed later than 3.0 a.m.   Upon reaching
their destination the hives should be treated as before shewn
after a journey.

### The Supers should Travel separated

from the hives, and be arranged in position on the next day
after the bees have been liberated or on the same day, as soon
as the bees are settled, if inconvenient to attend next day.
Each stock should have an extra chamber for better ventilation, and all openings for the admission of air must be shaded,
so that there may be as little excitement as possible to exhaust
the bees.

### My "Tenth" Method

of providing a young queen for *every* hive *yearly*; uniting at the
right time; *i.e.*, before feeding up where there is no late
harvest, or just before a late gathering is expected, will also
prove invaluable in many places in the States of America and
other localities where the gathering of stores so late as Sep-

tember, and sometimes in October, leaves the bees totally unfit to stand the rigours of winter, through the queen that has been used all the season failing to keep up the necessary supply of young bees.

The young queens are not to be raised before July, while in some instances it may be desirable to have them come on in August when the last flow is extra late.

After uniting, the capacity of ten or eleven, standard frames only should be allowed at this date, and no empty chamber will be required under or in front of the same, as no swarms will issue with the young queens.

## Another Plan.

Where one will not take the trouble to raise young queens for the purpose, and desires to make use of the heather honey stored in the stock combs, such must be removed one or two at a time and placed in another chamber below the brood nest after having the cappings sliced off, when the stores will be carried above provided the sections are filled, not with foundation, but combs already drawn out. In long hives such removed combs should be placed behind the division board.

## CHAPTER XXIII.

# DRIVEN BEES.

WHERE these can be secured in Autumn the general rules laid down for management of ordinary stock will of course apply in their case.

There are, however, a few minor matters that require attention, especially by those who have had no practice in this undertaking. Where the surrounding cottagers are willing to part with their bees instead of killing them, the general way is for the bar-framist to have them for his trouble, but on no occasion should he give more than 1s. for each lot, or they may turn out a dear bargain.

### How to Carry the Bees.

By using lightly-made straw skeps, the bee-keeper can carry eight or nine around his shoulder, slung on a broad strap. Thus by uniting, after driving, two or three lots into one, I have been able to carry home the bees from a large number of cottagers' skeps, over a distance of four or five miles where no trap could go. When a conveyance can be taken, light well-ventilated boxes can be used to greater advantage.

As soon as the bees are driven from their combs, secure them at once by tying a porous cloth over the mouth of the skep ; and when two or three are to be placed together, let them be united as soon as driven, first securing the queens not wanted that a young one may preside. If there is any use for other surplus young queens, place such in Benton cages with a dozen or more workers each.

## The Novice

should always begin by driving a skep or two of his own at home, and never attempt to practise first on the property of others, not only for the sake of his neighbour, but for his own and that of bee-keeping generally. After some experience in driving, then Mr. Lyon's " Bumping " process can be followed to advantage in many cases, though driving will often be more satisfactory, as being less inducive to robbing, there being no broken honey to excite the bees.

Mr. Lyon advises that all hives not being operated upon are to have their entrances closed with a bunch of grass inserted lightly, that ventilation may not be impeded. Where an outhouse can be utilized, however, there is no need for this operation.

Attention has already been called to

## Foul Brood,

and the bee-keeper should be on the watch for this when he may be taking bees. Where found the bees will be perfectly useless, as probably it would have developed during the spring, and the remaining occupants of the hive will not pay for their carriage home. Tell the owner of the condition of his bees and get him to smother them the same evening by the old plan, both for his own sake and the benefit of his neighbours. The whole skep must be burned ; and do not fail to impress him with the importance of leaving none of the honey in any way exposed.

## When to Hive the Bees.

One is so often told that it is necessary to place the bees in their new hive the same evening they are brought home, that I think it necessary to shew how robbing need not occur, even if combs wet from extracting are given to them at the middle of a warm day. It is considered that when put in during the evening all the bees congregate to the hive, but they would not in the daytime, besides being liable to get robbed out.

The fact is, with cool evenings often experienced in autumn, many bees are lost by their not being able to note their location ; whereas in the middle of the day they gradually settle down to the one spot like a new swarm and not one is lost, while the bee-keeper is able to find his extra queens, and is in no trouble about darkness coming upon him before he has half finished.

## Place the Frame-hives in Position,

quite empty, and shoot in the bees, taking care that only one queen is left to preside over the two, three, or more lots united. Now get your stored combs, or those fresh from the extractor, and arrànge them in position ; put on the quilt and cover all securely, leaving the entrance several inches wide. As the stored combs are given just before closing no robber bees are on hand ; but where empty combs or foundation have to be inserted, feed carefully until the hive is well supplied.

Taking average lots, the number to put together to make a fair stock should be as follows, according to the manner in which their house may be furnished—with stored combs, two swarms ; with empty combs, three ; foundation, four.

## Uniting to other Stocks.

A wasteful plan, which results only in loss of bees and time, is that of adding driven bees to weak colonies at home.

Without considering that fighting is almost certain to cause the death of thousands in the hands of many bee-keepers, but too frequently these bees only die out before winter is half over, leaving the stock worse off than before.

To be in any way satisfactory for this purpose the driven bees must first be made to develop a fair-sized brood nest in another hive on the spare combs of such lot ; when plenty of young bees are hatching *then* unite to your weak lot, saving the queen most to be desired. Feed and prepare for winter as hitherto shewn.

CHAPTER XXIV.

# HONEY, AND SOME OF ITS USES.

H ONEY is a wonderful gift of nature, and stands almost
alone as a pure natural sweet, perfect in itself.   There
are very many who have the impression that bees *make* honey;
but this is far from being the case.   Flowers *secrete* nectar
under the chemical action of the atmosphere upon the juices
of the plant, and this process is continued daily until the bee
while *gathering* such production is the means of mixing the
pollen of different flowers, almost invariably of the same kind,
and thus being fertilised and the plant made capable of repro-
duction by seeding, the object of the sweet attraction is
accomplished ;   the   flower   fades,   and   the   nectaries   are
dried   up.

### The Crude Nectar,

on being disgorged by the bee from its honey stomach, has
then imparted to it its remarkable preservative quality in the
shape of a minute proportion of formic acid.   Even now it does
not form honey as we use it.   The newly gathered liquid is
distributed over as large a comb surface as the number of
vacant cells will allow ; and thereafter the heat and ventilation afforded by the prosperous condition of the colony at the
time, together with the constant circulation of air maintained
in a systematic manner by the vibration of their wings kept

up by a regular force of workers, in due time ensure the evaporation of all excess of moisture. The honey then being ripened is gradually shifted to the upper and outer margins of the combs, where the cells are being purposely lengthened for storage (or to the super space when provided), and ultimately capped over, as filled.

## Medicinal Qualities.

Honey requires no digestion, but enters immediately into the system ; it is productive of heat, and by its regular use, the entire organism is benefited in a high degree, as it not only stimulates the appetite and aids digestion, but is at the same time better than any medicine for regulating the system.

Persons inclined to be costive, especially children, will find honey restore them to a perfectly normal condition ; while the continued use of purging medicines on the other hand causes a distressing reaction, because each dose impairs the delicate membrane of the stomach ; whereas the only rational course to pursue is to endeavour to restore the injured or relaxed parts.

Consumptives have received great benefit from the con-stant use of honey. Instances are on record where persons have been quite cured by it ; while others past all hope of recovery have enjoyed many years of life they had ceased to hope for or expect.

In that honey aids digestion, it of course gives healthy action to the liver, purifies the blood, and improves the general health.

A very distressing malady which will seldom yield to allopathic treatment is that known as "gravel." Honey taken daily will soon effect a cure, and I am quite sure those tor-tured with this complaint will not fail to avail themselves of such a simple remedy.

For colds, coughs, and sore throats, I suppose there is hardly a household but has had some experience with the use of honey either alone, or mixed with vinegar, lemon juice, or even butter, in case the palate does not appreciate the pure article alone; but for

## Definite Treatment

the following instructions, if carefully carried out, will prove. more efficacious than any system of drugging, because 'Nature' is judiciously assisted in her well-known endeavors to throw off disease; whereas drugs frequently check this attempt, or destroy life entirely.

In the first place, judging from the manner in which honey is generally applied, it is necessary to bring thick ripened honey to a gentle heat after adding a little boiled water. Whether granulated or not, and particularly if in the former condition, full benefit cannot be derived from its use until the honey has been brought back to the same condition as when first sealed up by the bees, and a tablespoonful of water to one pound of honey will generally be sufficient. Newly-extracted honey needs no addition of water, when used at once, as part of it comes from uncapped cells, from which the excess of moisture has not been removed.

## For Sore Throat and Night Cough

mix the juice of one good lemon with one pound of honey, stir thoroughly, and take of this one or two teaspoonsful frequently in connection with the following soothing and always beneficial treatment. At night, upon retiring to rest, fold a large linen handkerchief, and wring it out of tepid water; lay this right round the throat, and over that several folds of dry flannel. The latter keeps up internal warmth and materially assists in the speedy restoration of a normal condition of the throat. Do not remove the throat packing until rising, and then wash thoroughly with soap and water, cold by preference, but tepid if the person has a weak constitution.

In serious cases of night coughing, take the lemon honey night and day, and upon retiring to rest procure a jug holding about two quarts of boiling water. Sit up in bed and inhale the steam with the mouth open, continuing for ten or fifteen minutes, according to the strength of the patient, who must at the time be completely covered with a blanket, or mackintosh sheet by preference, that the steam may be retained. Wipe dry after, and lie down; repeating the process each night until relieved. Adopt the throat packing also if troublesome. For

## Bronchitis,

or severe cold on the lungs, especially in children, the supplementary treatment should be :—Bran poultices on back and chest, put on not too hot, and changed every twelve hours for the first day or two; then use them only each other six hours. It is imperative that several folds of dry flannel be wound round and across the shoulders and chest, over the poultices, as well as when they are not in use; and the body must be carefully and quickly washed with warm water-(and soap) at every change of the poultices. Keep in one room with a fire and the temperature at 60°; also have the bronchitis kettle steaming all the time.

## Honey as Food.

Though the sweetest of all sweets, honey is not suitable for cooking purposes in such a general manner as sugar, requiring a much larger quantity to sweeten many articles of food, as well as being more costly. There are many things, however, which are much improved by the addition of honey, such as fruit pies or puddings, cakes, &c.; while a basin of bread and milk is made very palatable when sweetened with it.

The following are among many excellent recipes given in Mr. T. G. Newman's "*Honey as Food and Medicine.*"

"Extracted honey is superior in every way for preserving fruit. Add one-third as much honey as fruit, boiling until the taste of the honey has evaporated.

"Those engaged in harvesting and other occupations tending to create thirst, will find the following preparation a very palatable and healthful drink in hot weather :—Take 12 gallons of water, 20 lbs. of honey, and the white of 6 eggs. Boil one hour ; then add cinnamon, ginger, cloves, mace, and a little rosemary. When cold add a spoonful of yeast from the brewery. Stir well, and in twenty-four hours it will be ready for use.

"For cooking green fruit use only extracted honey, which being the only liquid, holds the fruit firm and gives a very rich flavour. Sweeten or season with spices to suit the taste, and cook slowly until done. Serve dried fruit the same, only adding enough water to swell the fruit.

"To make Ginger Honey Cake, take 1¾ lbs. of honey, ¼ lb. of butter, 1½ lbs. of flour, 1 ounce of ginger, ½ ounce ground allspice, 1 teaspoonful of carbonate of soda, quarter of a pint of sour milk, cream if you choose, 3 eggs ; put the flour into a basin with the ginger and allspice ; mix these together, warm the butter and add it with the honey to the other ingredients ; stir well ; make the milk just warm and dissolve the soda in it, and make the whole into a nice smooth paste with the eggs which should be previously well whisked. Pour the mixture into a buttered tin ; bake it from three-quarters to one hour ; take the white of 1 egg and beat it up with a little sweet milk, then brush the same over the top with a feather to give it a glossy appearance.

"Honey Sponge Cake is nice eaten warm, and consists of two-thirds of a breakfast cup of sour cream, 3 of flour, an even teaspoonful of soda, 1 cup of butter, 3 eggs, 1¼ lbs. of honey, 1 tablespoonful of cinnamon, ¼ ditto of allspice, and a little extract of lemon ; mix the spices with the flour ; put the soda in the milk and stir well, that all the ingredients may thoroughly mix ; beat the cake well for another five minutes ; put it in a buttered tin—bake from one-half to three-quarters-of-an-hour.

" Butter Honey Cake is pronounced by all to be excellent. One pint of flour, 1 tablespoonful of butter, 1 teaspoonful of soda, 2 ditto of cream of tartar, and honey sufficient to make a thick batter. Spread out an inch thick, and bake in a hot oven.

" To make Mead, not inferior to the best foreign wines, put 3 lbs. of the finest honey to two gallons of water, two lemon peels to each gallon; boil it half-an-hour, and skim well. Put in the peel while boiling. Work this mixture with yeast, and then put it in a vessel to stand five or six months, when bottle for use. If desired to keep it for several years, add four pounds of honey to a gallon of water.

" A cheap Honey Tea Cake is made with one teacup of extracted honey, half ditto of thick sour cream, 2 eggs, half teacup of butter, two of flour, scant half teaspoon of soda, one ditto of cream of tartar; flavour to taste.

METHEGLIN.—" Mix honey and water strong enough to carry an egg; let it stand three or four weeks in a warm place to ferment; then drain through a cloth, and add spices to suit the taste.

" Honey Vinegar is obtained as follows :—Heat 30 gallons of rain-water and put it into a barrel; add two quarts of whisky, three pounds of honey, three-pennyworth of citric acid, and a little mother of vinegar. Fasten up the barrel, place it in the cellar, and in a short time it will contain vinegar unsurpassed for purity and excellence of taste."

Mr. Allan Pringle gives a substitute for tea and coffee :— Take three quarts of good, clean, wheat bran; and bake in the oven till it becomes quite brown. Then add one quart of liquid honey and stir thoroughly; put it back in the oven to bake still more, stirring it frequently until it gets dry, granulated and very brown. Draw it the same as coffee and use with milk and honey, or milk and sugar to suit taste.

Honey-Lemonade.—Make it in the usual way, using honey instead of sugar; nothing can be used as a summer beverage that is more grateful and refreshing. Try it. Many thousands of pounds of honey may be used in this way, and all the users be benefited.—*British Bee Journal.*

## General Uses.

Besides the foregoing, honey is used in preparations for preserving leather; in ointments for various purposes, such as for chapped hands, sores, &c.; and is very largely used by chemists in their many preparations. For printers' rollers it takes the place of sugar, doing better work, and making a more durable article.

The reader will thus see that honey is not simply an article of luxury, nor of ordinary diet; and instead of bee-keepers complaining that there is little demand for their produce, let each endeavour to find some new use for it; and thus make an opening for the consumption of honey by the ton, where otherwise it would never have been thought of.

A large firm of biscuit makers were induced to start a new biscuit sweetened with honey, and thereupon required two tons of the bees' product weekly. Though we may not often find an opening for it to this extent, there are many ways in which honey is, and can be disposed of, other than for table use.

CHAPTER XXV.

# WORKING TWO QUEENS IN ONE HIVE.

## THE WELLS' SYSTEM.

A FEW years back Dr. Stroud, of South Africa, mentioned in the *British Bee Journal* that he had a system of working any number of queens in one hive or colony, and that he had long practised that method. . No details, however, were given by him, and if there were any merits in his process he appears to have been careful to keep the supposed secret to himself.

A more recent correspondent makes in the same journal a statement to the effect that he had saved five queens over winter in one colony of bees, all having free access to the respective queens. This is no more than has been known to, and carried out by many other bee-keepers, especially in the process of modern queen-rearing. Mr. Heddon, of Dowagiac, Michigan, laid claim to being first to point out the possibility of working more than one queen in a hive : Doolittle and

Q

others made some practical demonstration of the fact, but neither of them preceded Dr. Stroud. Simple tiering hives were used for the purpose in America, similar to Fig. 63, but the plan was adopted solely for queen-rearing purposes. So far as is known, Mr. Wells, of Aylesford, has been the first to reduce the matter to practical working as a system in *honey pro-duction*. The entire correspondence upon the subject will be found in the *British Bee Journal* of the current year and in the issue of November 10th, 1892, after stating he had made up his mind to work none but 'two-queen' colonies in future, upon further consideration and in deference to other expressed opinions, he says : " In order to compare results, and make the matter as plain as possible, I decided to change my plans, and work five single-queened stocks through the season, and very carefully note results. It will, perhaps, not be out of place just to say once more that the double stocks have two queens in each [one queen in each brood chamber], divided in centre of hive with the thin wood perforated dummy, so that neither queen nor bees can pass beyond their own part of the hive ; but at supering-time a sheet of queen-excluder zinc is placed on top of the frames, and on this the super, into which *both* lots of bees are allowed to run and mix together as they please. . . . . . Most of my hives hold fourteen standard frames, though I consider a hive of this size is not large enough for the two queens, and so when more room is wanted for brood, I put a box of shallow frames, with a thin solid dummy in centre, exactly *over* the perforated one below. This I thought would give plenty of breeding room, and I wished to prevent swarming as much as possible. I have not, however, made a success of that part of the business yet. . : . . . . The five double hives gave 762 lbs. surplus extracted, and 27 lbs. surplus sections ; total, 789 lbs. The five single queen hives 205 lbs. ; or a grand total from all the hives of 994 lbs."

The figures showing the financial situation for the year, given by such a practical and painstaking apiarist as

Mr. Wells, will be of considerable interest, and are as follows :—

|  |  |  | £ | *s.* | *d.* |
|---|---|---|---|---|---|
| 940 lbs. extracted honey at 8d. | ... | 31 | 6 | 8 |
| 54 „ comb „ „ 1/- | ... | 2 | 14 | 0 |
| 30 „ wax „ 2/- | ... | 3 | 0 | 0 |
|  |  |  | 37 | 0 | 8 |
| Total expenditure | ... | 5 | 1 | 10 |
| Balance... ... ... | £31 | 18 | 10 |

Mr. Wells considered the season below the average, but besides the above balance of profit he had a lot of surplus brood combs left over, either empty or partly stored; and these form one of the most valuable ' stock-in-trade ' adjuncts. of the apiary.

Mr. Wells will doubtless adopt a hive which will give him more room, as well as aid in prevention of swarming, but in the absence of any further particulars I give several illustrations of a hive which I think will meet the case and help to more clearly explain the process, while the addition of my ' safety-valve ' or non-swarming chamber UNDER the brood nest must largely assist in disposing of the trouble complained of, as well as dispense with the need of a dropping floor.

## The Illustrations

shew (Fig. 60) the double brood chamber, A, with the perforated division board, P D, between, and the non-swarming arrangement under, having a perfectly plain, tight-fitting division board, D, between the two compartments, B B, and fitting close to, and immediately under, the perforated board. The hive allows nine frames on either side, and with the frames below having starters only there will be little inclination to swarm when the supers also are in position.

The perforated dividing board is thus described by Mr. Wells: . . . . " The kind of wood I use is the best yellow pine, about ¼-inch thick, shoulders projecting the same depth as the thickness of top bar of frames used . . . so as to be level with top of frames when in position. Warping is prevented by folding a strip of light tin around the ends, leaving a small piece long enough to turn over top and bottom. I make holes first with a bradawl, then run a hot iron through about ¼-inch thick, each hole being about ¼-inch apart."

A board of soft wood so thin as ⅛-th of an inch will soon be rendered useless for the purpose, as bees have a peculiar habit of continually scraping and biting and will in time make openings large enough to pass through. It seems therefore advisable either to use harder wood or a slightly thicker board. Moreover, a thin board as a divider is very inconvenient, and will doubtless be far more useful and permanent if itself let into a broader rim forming a close-fitting frame as illustrated.

## The Perforated Zinc

may or may not be secured in a frame, but the frame shewn under the super crate in Fig. 61 appears to me the better way of using it. The centre stay, P, is the same thickness as the rim, and in these pieces the zinc is secured by running into a saw-cut made along the centre of the edges. The stays, H H, are only half thickness, the zinc being fastened to the under-. side of these and thus keeping all clear of the frames.

## The Super Crate

is arranged so that through and free communication is to be had from end to end (Fig. 61), though it is probable that the divisional super in three separate crates of full length will be found more convenient than one heavy crate.

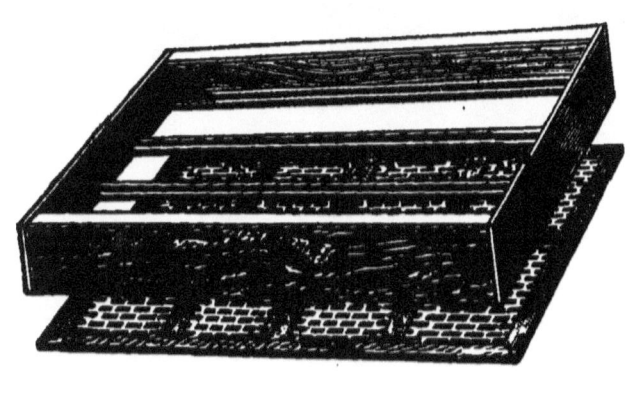

Fig. 61.
Queen Excluder, fitted in frame, shewn under double super crate.

Fig. 60.
Double Hive, with Wells' Perforated Divider between, P D; shewn with Simmins' Non-swarming Chamber under.

## The Floor

is secured to, and rests upon, two pieces of stout deal, 3-inch by 2-inch, while the alighting boards are each set under the main level; thus a full width entrance is allowed, and is regulated by simple wood blocks as shewn at **E**.

By using the frame all round the thin perforated dummy, the floor board can be made in two separate pieces, and hinged to a centre strip across the bottom, and thus the supposed advantage of slanting the floor can be carried out on either side with no disturbance to the other, and the far more convenient form of opposite and distinct entrances retained. In this case, legs can be secured to the stand as in Fig. 62. I do not myself see the necessity of a dropping floor, but there are doubtless others who will be pleased to know how to carry out Mr. Wells' plan without the sad inconvenience of legs fastened to the body of the brood chamber.

For commercial purposes, plinths around the rims of hives are found unnecessary, as also are porches, but these can be added to suit the tastes of those who require such.

## The Trouble in case of Swarming

will probably be the greatest difficulty to contend with, as the two queens must go out with the double swarm; but this difficulty will be entirely overcome by adopting my swarm catcher to each compartment, thus retaining each queen under her original brood chamber, and after the removal of the surplus queen cells, work will go on merrily again.

## The Disadvantages of the System

are: The extra labour required throughout, as well as more cumbersome hives; the use of perforated zinc being also a necessity; while the greater inclination to swarm, together with the fact that both lots with their respective queens go out

at the same time, will sadly inconvenience many who attempt
to carry out the plan.

## The Comparative Advantages.

At first sight, to many bee-keepers, the 'dual' plan appears
to give extraordinary results; but it must not be forgotten
that there are two stocks working together.  Thus the average
of, say 160 lbs., if divided between the two will be 80 lbs. only
for each stock, and that nearly all *extracted* honey.   It is no
unusual thing for a single-queen stock to produce from 80 lbs.
to 100 lbs. of *comb honey* during an average season.   But in an
apiary run for honey alone the practical bee-keeper carries out
the well-known

## Doubling System

and secures far better results from the population of two
colonies thrown with *one* queen than can be shewn by the
twin hive system; while the hive is far more simple, there
need be no perforated zinc used, and, moreover, there is less
fear of swarming.   The Wells' plan can hardly stand against
the more simple and reliable practice which many bee-keepers
seem to have lost sight of, but it should at least bring more
forcibly to their notice the undeniable fact that *none but the most
powerful colonies are really profitable*, and that because at the
right time the working force is far in excess of the number of
young who require constant attention and make heavy
demands upon the incoming stores.

## Working two or more Queens in Storifying Hives.

Having so far considered the plan of working two stocks
together on the same floor, I shall not be doing justice to my
readers if I leave them without shewing how not only two,
but any number, of queens may be worked in a far more
simple manner on the storifying plan; so that those using the

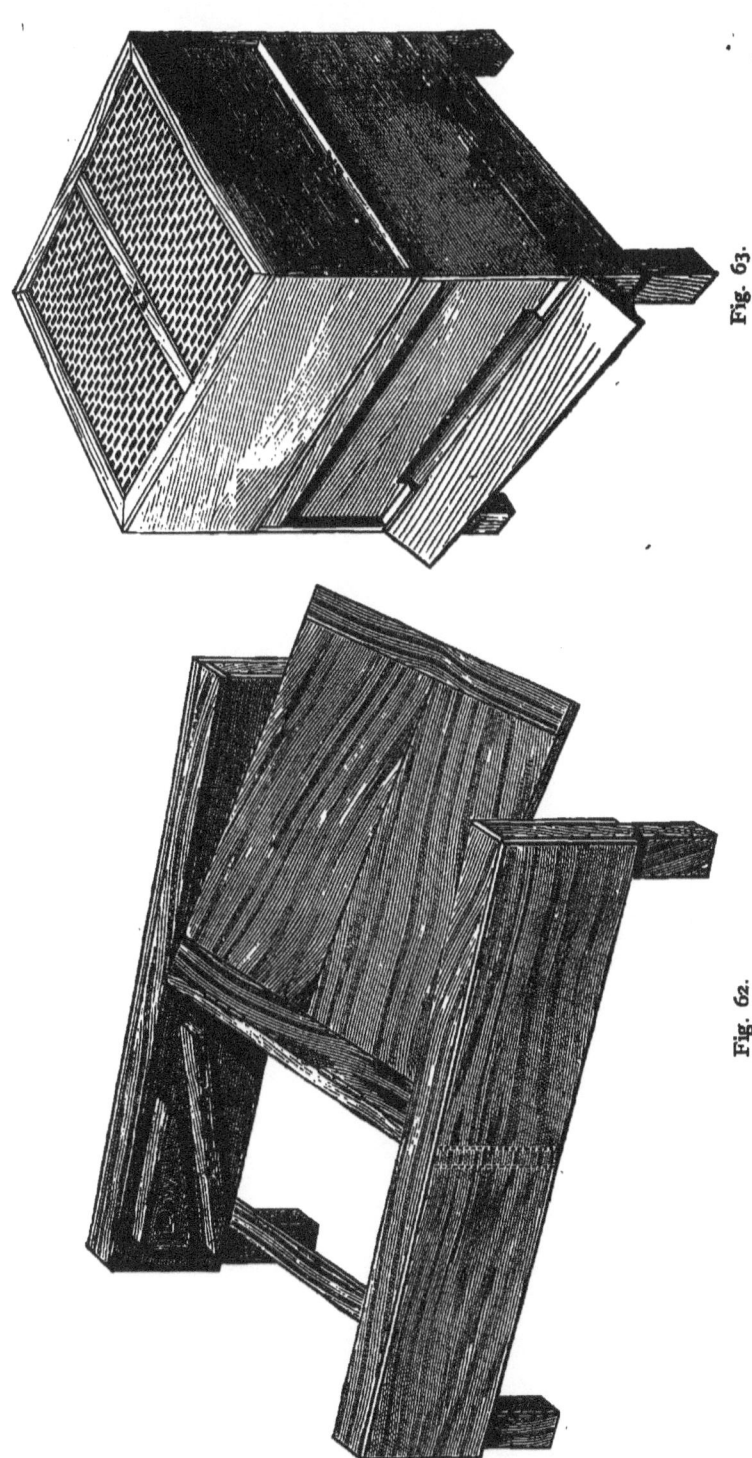

Fig. 63.

Manner of working two or more Queens on the
tiering plan.

Fig. 62.

Double Stand, with Dropping Floor to each side;. the legs fixed only to the stand.
W the wedge for securing floor.

lighter hive need not go to much expense in giving the method a trial, and need not alter their existing hives in the least.

With populous colonies there is no advantage in wintering two clusters of bees close together, though it may be done with the smaller hive if desired. The extra furniture required will be a small-hole perforated divider, placed as an adapter between each brood chamber until the bees are considered mutually good tempered. These boards will then be removed and excluder zinc adapters inserted. The entrances to both may remain open, or the lower one only left, as found most convenient. In the latter case it will be observed that where the lower chamber is provided for prevention of swarming, and a queen excluding board also placed between it and the first brood chamber, that the queens are each confined to their own compartment, and can not be lost even if the bees do on any occasion swarm out.

My own objection to perforated zinc has been explained again and again, and I am prepared to assert that better results are to be obtained without its use. One good queen can supply more brood than is generally wanted, and the whole question turns simply upon the proper amalgamation of forces at the right time.

## Dropping Floors.

Mr. Wells considered his hives were not quite suitable for working double stocks, and therefore one can not be surprised to find him advocating a floor such as was generally fitted to the first bar-frame hives introduced, with legs attached to the walls. The floor was secured by means of long wedge-like pieces of wood inserted at each side, and when these were removed of course it dropped directly upon the ledges. The only reason why Mr. Wells appears to require this dropping floor is to accommodate an excess of bees just after uniting any two stocks into one, but this requisition simply shews three serious defects in the method of working. First, as he himself has already pointed out, his brood nest was not large enough ; next, no legs should ever be fastened to the hive proper; and lastly, the fact was overlooked that by adopting my non-swarming chamber *under* the brood nest ample room is given for any quantity of bees. In the face of these facts, therefore, it seems useless to give an illustration of a pattern which has long since been discarded by practical bee-keepers ; as legs fixed to the stock hive form the most serious obstacle to profitable bee-keeping.

This is so well understood in America that one might search the States and Canada through and not find one per cent. of the hives with anything approaching legs attached to the stock hive.

## A Caution.

There is one item with regard to Mr. Wells' system which does not appear to have been noticed. It should be remembered that the supers being removed, he immediately closes the upper part of the hive by replacing the quilting, and thus there are again two separate stocks. Should the supers remain until late in the year, or the two queens be left at the heather, the almost certain result will be that the bees unite into one body on one side of the division board, and at the same time destroy or leave the other queen to her fate. The same will also occur, as the cold nights approach, with the hive tiered up, with two or more queens, as shewn in Fig. 63 ; and, therefore, upon removal of surplus chambers, the respective colonies must be divided if it is desired to keep them distinct ; or the small-hole dividers can be replaced between the different body boxes. Where this

## Tiering-up Plan

is followed the small-hole perforated wood or zinc is to be used between the respective storeys for a few days, and then its place taken by the ordinary queen-excluder, as shewn in the illustration. Mr. Wells considers the queens will fight with only the ordinary excluder zinc between them, but he overlooks the fact that queens once fertilised never fight, and if they attempted so to do could not injure each other because the sting then becomes useless. I have had as many as a dozen fertilised queens all in one compartment without injury to either; but the result with virgin queens, under such a condition, would have been death to all but one in a very few minutes.

# NOTES BY THE WAY.

Dear Reader, to enable you the better to succeed, set up a standard of perfection that you wish to attain in your management. Never mind if it appears almost impossible to gain that end; if you will only keep the desired object in view, and work earnestly, depend upon it you will be almost certain to reach your goal.

---

In these days there are so many ladies looking out for an occupation which will be helpful in meeting the general expenses at home, that the subject of modern bee-keeping must be one that will command greater attention from the gentler sex in the future.

---

If in possession of a small space of garden ground a few hives of bees can be cultivated in a manner that will bring a handsome profit and a delightful sense of independence to the happy owner of the industrious workers.

---

In the absence of a garden plot, bees may be placed in cabinet hives—two to a window—inside of any room which does not face a main street; and thus protected will do better than outside.

There is not the slightest sense of degradation attached to the occupation. It is in every respect a soul-inspiring and intensely interesting study, followed by hundreds of cultured people.

---

Bees are never idle except from sheer force of circumstances; and what do you think they do in winter? When it is very cold they simply cluster in one compact mass; but with each returning spell of milder weather this living ball expands, and many of the little insects travel to and from the most distant sealed combs of honey, and commencing on the outer surface of each outside comb the whole of the honey there stored is carried to those cells in close contact with the cluster. Though this process is repeated as often as opportunity occurs, there is no variation in the manner of proceeding, for the food in the intermediate combs is never disturbed until its turn comes in due order for clearance.

---

Now I will tell you of the best swarm catcher, the most simple and the least expensive; indeed it costs nothing and is not new either. Just think of all the clap-traps on this and the other side of the 'big pond,' and you may well ask why bee-keepers are running after these expensive swarm-catching fads when by simply *clipping the wings* of the queens the whole question is popped into a nutshell.

---

Pick your queen up in the left hand; hold her firmly but gently between the thumb and forefingers, and with a pair of small sharp scissors clip off a small portion of the larger wing on one side. She will never lead a swarm away, and the bees will return to the mother hive as surely as if the complicated traps were in use.

Mr. S. Deacon, of Knysna, Cape of Good Hope, in a letter dated Nov. 23rd, 1892, says, " I am a struggling apiarist, and can fully endorse your statement at bottom of Page 1 of your *immensely* valuable and *valued* little work, " A Modern Bee Farm." I and my son (a regular bee enthusiast, aged 18) are agreed that it is worth its weight in gold! I should certainly be sorry to take £5 for the copy I have just received from home if I knew it were impossible to obtain another. ——, ——, ——, ——, and some half-a-dozen others, who have sought to teach us our business, can in future rest on the shelves! There are a thousand and one little matters we have in vain sought information on in the works of the authors above-named. They *generalize*, but the novice wants *details*. . . . . I am not going to waste any more money on bee books, convinced that what Simmins' work doesn't teach us isn't worth knowing! . . . . for really I can not say enough in praise of your book."

---

The above gentleman reminds me he has a trouble I have not mentioned in my work. He complains that it is the rule, rather than the exception, for the bees out there to leave their hives and combs—every bee deserting and going off like a swarm. Once in a while a similar thing happens in this climate, where, through inattention, the bees have not been properly supplied with stores. These swarms are called "starvation" swarms.

---

It may be that Mr. Deacon thought feeding unnecessary in his locality, but as he states that the combs deserted are perfectly empty, it points to the fact that the bees were arriving at the starvation point, and made the one desperate effort in the hope of finding more favourable pastures.

It should never be forgotten that whether bees are situated in a hot or cold climate, the period equal to a winter's rest is an absolute necessity. But the necessary quietude for ensuring the benefits of that period is only to be attained when the bees find themselves in possession of an abundance of sealed food.

Indeed, in the warmer climate even more food is required, as there is likely to be a longer period of activity before the main honey harvest actually comes on, and without the stored food to fall back upon, the aged bees wear themselves out, without attempting to rear a younger population to succeed them. Hence it is quite possible a colony may in some cases die right out; and such deaths occurring on the wing, a not too observant beekeeper may well think his bees have swarmed out.

California is considered the Bee-keeper's paradise, and probably there is no other place on the face of the earth where bee-keeping is carried on so generally, and on the other hand, no country where so many bees die out wholesale. This is both because some of the bee-keepers, relying upon the generally favourable climate, rob their bees too close, and neglect to feed when a dull time arrives.

The general rules for bee-culture extend to all climes, but when we hear of bees in warm climates yielding comparatively light surplus stores, or even becoming idle, and not working at all, it simply points to the conclusion that the owner does not pay proper attention to their management. While there they require more stores to fall back upon during the time of rest than is wanted in the coldest localities; when honey does come in, it must be removed quickly, and an enormous comb space allowed for its daily storage.

R

On the other hand, in the absence of surplus combs or space, the queens are crowded out, little or no brood rearing can be carried on, and then with no young workers, we meet the opposite extreme—the older workers must die off—this time leaving a fully-stored hive, instead of empty combs.

Under very favourable conditions, even with all possible storage room, the brood nest cannot be extended sufficiently, to make up for the wear and tear of bee-life. Thus we see the reason why a district capable of producing 400 or 500 pounds of honey annually per colony, seldom gives as much as 200, more frequently considerably less.

Under these circumstances, nothing but a judicious system of combined division and re-uniting—keeping up the brood supply with the young bees and young queen—will ever give results fully equal to the resources of the district.

During a heavy flow bees will unite anyhow, therefore select any two colonies standing near together; unite the whole of the bees and brood in one of the two, excepting such as return to the empty hive with the queen. Fill this with frames of foundation, or having starters only attached to the top bars. This new swarm will soon fill up with brood and store.

But our object is to ensure that this new swarm rears a *continuous supply of brood and bees.* Meanwhile, bring it within a foot or so of the hive, which has already received its combs and adhering bees. After three weeks remove the new swarm quite behind the other, and the latter will then receive all the flying bees. After a day or two shift the new lot to the opposite side, always standing a little back, but facing the same way as the larger stock.

By shifting this breeding stock as often as it is found the bees are increasing and working sufficiently to crowd the queen, her hive then always has a population capable of *nursing* rather than storing, while the main working hive has a constant renewal of young workers, without the usual trouble of uniting and changing surplus receptacles. The queen in the main working stock has very little room for breeding, while there is little inclination to swarm. It is the nearest approach I know of for practically working a colony without a laying queen, with none of its disadvantages, while there is a continuous supply of young bees from the companion hive.

Young queens can be secured from the breeding stock, while combs of brood from the same are used for the nuclei ; and the young queen, when mated, exchanged at a convenient opportunity. In case of swarming, work the new swarm alone until a young queen is mated and laying, and then re-unite after deposing the old queen as already shewn ; bu when the non-swarming chamber is used that trouble wi seldom arise.

Notwithstanding that hot thick syrup in cases of emergency is better in cold weather than candy, it must not be supplied in large quantities. Three or four pounds given all at once is sufficient, and will carry any needy colony through until the middle of February, when feeding can be more satisfactorily carried on.

But, frequently, is there any need to feed at all at un-seasonable times ? If there is a fair amount of sealed stores in November, far better leave the bees alone until February.

From November to February, bees make but little impression upon their stores ; but as soon as breeding is on the way a difference can be seen, and it is from that time forward where the real danger lies and when bees are most frequently neglected.

---

On the other hand, where bees go into winter with the combs heavily charged with unsealed syrup given late in the year, they can not possibly cluster in a compact body, and being divided into thin seams they soon succumb to the additional cold caused by the unsealed food all among them.

---

If syrup feeding in winter is a necessity it is better to take advantage of a warm spell and slip in one or two empty frames so that the bees may cluster in large masses ; indeed, it is advisable in any case to prepare stocks for winter in this manner.

---

Let it be considered that during cold weather the combs are really *unnecessary* except as the store cupboards.   Under normal conditions, during late autumn, at the central lower portion of the combs the cells are all empty, just as vacated by the later batches of brood.   As the cold weather comes on the bees form upon that portion of the combs, the nearest possible approach to a perfectly unbroken cluster.   Some of them occupy the empty cells and rest head to head on opposite sides of the centre wall of the combs, while others crowd between.

---

Thus they make the best of the situation as they find it ; but careful experiments conducted over a series of years have always shewn me that the bees prefer to cluster in winter where there are no combs at all to intersect them, and in this situation have less difficulty in maintaining that animal heat so necessary for the preservation of life.

---

We can therefore meet them half-way as it were, and while not removing the stores can alternate heavy combs with empty frames, thus bringing the cluster into a more compact mass, and entirely avoiding the frequent destruction of the unfortunate outer seams of bees.

---

Mr. Wells shews 994 lbs. of honey (nearly all extracted) from five single hives and five double-queen stocks ; that is, from *fifteen* stocks in all. The dual queen system, therefore, with its more cumbersome and inconvenient hives does not compare favourably with the result of 1,360 lbs. obtained by Mr. Cowan from *seven* single-queen hives.

---

In 1874, Mr. Cowan also reported 907 lbs. from *twelve* hives, of which 707 lbs. were comb-honey.

---

In the following year, a very wet season, the same gentleman took the first prize at the Crystal Palace show for comb-honey taken from one colony and weighing 80½ lbs. ; besides this, 20 lbs. of extracted had also been removed from the same hive.

---

Just as the proportion of adult bees, before the opening of the season, exceeds those being nursed up to maturity, so may the prosperity of a colony be gauged. This does not imply that an already limited brood nest should be reduced by application of the fads generally proposed, but it points to the absolute fact that such disproportion should not have existed at all.

It has been considered that practical bee-keeping owes much to science, and that scientific bee-keeping owes little to practice. What is science but ascertained knowledge, gained by the continued practice of ages, the good being consolidated, while the chaff has been expelled? Correct practice alone constitutes and establishes true science.

---

By a careful experiment I have found there are 3,500 worker bees to the pound. Queens will live from three to four years; drones, three months; workers during summer, six weeks, and through the quiet months of winter six months.

---

Cyprian and Syrian queens are much smaller than those of either the Carniolan or native kinds. The drones also are smaller, consequently I find where only males of the larger races are flying, the Cyprian or Syrian queens are often long in finding a mate.

---

Whatever requires doing about the apiary should be done at once. If left for another day, an important matter is liable to be forgotten when many other things require attention, and considerable loss ensues. Where any need cannot be attended to immediately some note or sign must be made, but the apiarist should not make a note of every little detail that requires his attention, or such a course will only tend- to weaken the intellect.

---

Fertile workers are not often troublesome except in the queen-raising apiary. When they persist in laying in nuclei, do not attempt to give virgin queens, but at once supply a good fertile queen on a comb of brood, with accompanying bees; this also being the very best and simplest cure where they are found in stocks of greater strength. The worker deposits eggs in a very irregular manner, sometimes a dozen or more in one cell; but this must not be confused with the work of a young or prolific queen, which because of limited room or too small a number of bees will often lay several eggs in a cell.

------

Where eggs of fertile workers are placed in worker cells, many of the larvæ die before reaching maturity, otherwise the cappings are much raised above the surface, as with normal drones; and those that do hatch appear equally as perfect as the latter, though, of course, dwarfed in appearance.

------

While it is impossible for one to make a success of bee-keeping on an extensive scale if he has another "business" on hand which requires constant and regular attention, there are, of course, a number of light occupations that can be adopted to fill up one's spare time. If bee-keeping is a secondary consideration, then the bees must often be neglected at the most critical time, and loss consequently results. One may keep poultry to advantage, especially where certain crops are grown for the bees as elsewhere shown. A large apiary will keep the owner busy during the winter months preparing for the following season; but there are long evenings in winter, and other times when the want of some suitable work will be felt. Each must consider what is best suited to himself; what he can obtain; or what course of study may ultimately be of advantage to him. Something must be taken in hand that can be picked up at any opportunity and that can be laid down the moment the bees require attention. One may be at work during the usual hours of the day, but that is no reason why he should spend the remainder in idleness and frivolity. Not for a moment do I intend that a holiday should never be taken ; but a bee-keeper especially, though his work is often laborious, has a holiday every day ;. for is he not always in the open air, gaining health and strength, as well as having constant pleasure in studying the wonderful works of Nature ?

Many writers have fallen into the error of supposing that young queens often commence by laying a number of drone as well as worker eggs. In nuclei it is frequently to be noticed that many cells contain drone larvæ, but a little more careful observation will always show that this is the result of fertile workers, which often continue to deposit eggs after the young queen is in full work. I have even had these pests start laying side by side with a queen after she had been at work long enough to hatch her first batch of brood. The queen was a Carniolan crossed with black drone; the fertile worker was from a Ligurian queen crossed by Cyprian drone, the resulting drones being very yellow. The yellow bees had been united to the stock to strengthen it, and without this proof it might have been considered that the queen had produced the drones. Again, a queen does not deposit eggs until her ovaries are developed.

While I have had ample evidence to show that bees are able to retard the development of both eggs and larvæ by withholding food ; where a colony has been queenless for more than ten days, the presence of uncapped larvæ, whether in queen cell cups or ordinary cells, may be put down to the action of fertile workers.

Many bee-keepers appear to understand that my non-swarming plan can be carried out in a single ten or eleven-frame hive, allowing only two or three frames at the front with starters. I would never attempt such a pretence as this, and could not myself work with so little space. I must have longer hives and six or seven empty frames in front of the brood nest; or, in the case of ten-frame hives, another chamber having only starters must be placed under the brood nest, as distinctly pointed out in my Non-Swarming pamphlet, and now illustrated in the chapter on that subject.

---

Bees winter best with plenty of room below the frames. Many of my own stocks have been wintered with the lower body under the stock chamber, as used for prevention of swarming, with very satisfactory results.

---

Chickens will be found very serviceable in the apiary, as they destroy a large number of insects. Earwigs especially, and sometimes ants, swarm about the hives, but though they do no harm they are a great nuisance. Chickens turned down as soon as they can take care of themselves, can soon be taught to look in the right place for the pests, and will be on hand when the hives are opened.

---

With a quarter of an acre of borage, the seed from a number of sunflowers, and a good grass run, in all rather more than an acre, I have had about a dozen fowls come along fit for the table, with no other feeding, except a little corn for a week or ten days before killing.

---

None of the birds have been actually stung, though sometimes attacked. At first they simply pick off the bee; but finding their enemy returns to the charge, they soon learn how to settle it, and then invariably give the bee a sound grip before it can leave the ground.

While borage, melilot clover, and other plants may not be suitable for cattle, my own experience goes far to show that chickens can be brought up at little expense where they have admission to a large area of such plants, which throw suitable seed. Borage especially is very valuable, giving a constant supply for several months. Old birds must not have the run of the plants or they will pick off the bloom and cause waste by treading down the plants before they get a good growth.

Sunflowers cannot be considered suitable for bees, judging by half-an-acre grown as a test near one hundred colonies, when with fine weather the flowers were almost entirely neglected. Nothing else of importance was in reach of the bees at the time. The same area of melilot clover, in the same place, the following year, simply roared with bees.

The best show card I have been able to find for the retailer is an Observatory Hive, placed in the shop window. A single comb with bees and queen has proved to be a very great attraction, introducing new customers in quite an unlooked-for manner.

We know how distressing it is to see the usual observatory hives at bee exhibitions, with the insufficient ventilation and numbers of dead bees, resulting from overcrowding, but we want our bees to remain confined quite three weeks in good order, as it would be out of the question changing them every few days. I have had them in good condition for more than four weeks; and three weeks' confinement in the window with daily exposure with few stains to be seen.

The single-comb observatory is made as illustrated at Fig. 64, with a 3-inch space below the comb and three 1-inch holes both sides, covered on the inside with perforated zinc for

Fig. 64.
Single Comb Observatory Hive.

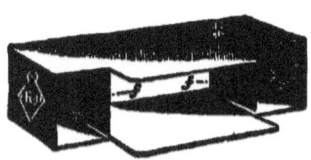

Fig. 65.
The " W. B. Carr " Metal End.

Fig. 66.
Abbott's Comb Honey
Exhibition Crate.

Fig. 67.
Spring Travelling Case for same.

Fig 68.
Simmins' Close-end Frame Hive (1878).

Fig. 69.
Frame Feeder, Self-acting
Process.

Fig. 70.
The inner portion of same,
shewing Perforated Sugar
Holder and Bee-passage.

thorough ventilation; while at the same time such darkened recess hides any refuse or dead bees that may drop from above. A comb should be selected not too light nor too dark, about half full of stores; not more than enough bees to cover one side of the comb; having no brood, but a nice yellow queen. If the bees are mostly young very few will die, as the window will be shaded from the sun, and before they are ready to be exchanged young bees are hatching out from the small patch of brood generally started. A suitable darkened crate with convenient handle must be provided for transit. As no brood is inserted in the first instance, this kind of adver-tising can be carried on in all but the coldest weather.

For exposition at Bee Shows the same arrangement would be found much more convenient than most of those used, and with fewer bees the observatory would be presentable for a much longer period.

The exhibition of bees for the purpose of obtaining prizes is but a farce, to say the least. The working qualities of the bees cannot be considered, and I will show how easily the judges may be deceived as to colour and markings. Whenever friends have asked my opinion about the preparation of bees for competition I have recommended the following course; and the result has justified my advice.

Whatever kind you intend to exhibit, see that they are all young bees placed in your observatory, and on a newly-built comb of brood; the framework to be painted a pale green in contrast to the light-coloured comb. The young bees are secured by making up a nucleus a few days before they are required, with plenty of hatching brood; most of the old workers returning to the original stand. It will readily be seen therefore that bees from inferior stock may thus gain the prize in competition with others not so prepared, though the latter may on the whole possess the better qualities.

·

---

The man who enters a large bee-farm for a term in the hope of gaining an insight into the practical management of the same, must not think all the necessary information is to be picked up simply by looking around and paying occasional visits to the apiary. On the contrary, he must make up his mind to go there to work just as any other apprentice or assistant. The daily routine must be gone through in every particular, and though some manipulations may be repeated constantly, it will be only by such close study and application that he will make himself master of the entire practical management.

---

Many inquire how they are to know when honey is coming in. Examination of the hive will, of course, show every vacant cell being more or less occupied with the thin newly-gathered nectar. The bees, too, come in with distended bodies, falling heavily upon the flight board. Sometimes the aroma of the incoming stores is distinctly noticeable, more particularly at evening when many bees are ventilating at the entrance, and a perfect roar is heard throughout the apiary. Apart from this, the advanced apiarist has an instinctive feeling that honey is, or is not, being gathered. The state of the atmosphere and his knowledge of surrounding crops tell him at once what to expect. The temperature may range anywhere from $70°$ to $90°$ in the shade, but if it continue too hot and dry for more than ten or fourteen days, the amount of honey brought in will decrease daily, unless there happen to be a succession of heavy ground crops coming along, when, the earth being shaded, moisture is still retained. A shower once in a while is beneficial, but frequent rainfalls destroy all chance of a good honey flow, as such induce also a low temperature. Even with fair weather it sometimes happens that the temperature rules too low for the secretion of nectar ; but usually if none is stored during a fine season, it implies either that the district is poor in honey plants, or else that there are too many colonies in one place.

The question of over-stocking is one that has received considerable attention, though nothing satisfactory has been arrived at in regard to this matter. It may safely be said, however, than in any fairly good district 100 colonies will each put out as much surplus as one only. But with a large number, however, there are greater risks, and the whole cannot receive the same attention individually that would be given to a few. It will generally be found that it is not the district which is at fault, but rather that our stocks are not always ready when the first or only glut of the season occurs. Honey is seldom secreted so abundantly as when everything is bursting into new life, but it so happens at that early date it is often difficult to get the bees strong enough to do much more than provide for the expanding brood nest. When bees can be so wintered that they will come out stronger in spring than when they settled down for winter, we shall hear little more about " over-stocking."

We are frequently told that drones are useful in keeping the brood warm ; but why raise drones, if not required for breeding, when in the same space of comb a larger number of workers could be produced, who would add to the prosperity of the hive instead of being useless consumers ? The statement is contradicted on the face of it, for why is it the drones

are present only when additional heat can be dispensed with ?
As a simple matter of fact, they have but one use, and that is
the fertilization of the young queens.

---

There are two important points in reference to feeding that
were first brought forward by Mr. Abbott, late editor of the
*British Bee Journal,* and which require careful consideration.
That veteran always insisted that to stimulate bees to extend
the brood nest when desired they must have a gentle *continuous*
supply.   Again, when it is necessary to supply food for winter
it should be given during the month of August, because the
bees are then better able to store and seal it.   Now, while we
may not all quite agree with the latter statement, there is
much of truth behind it.   Where there is no late harvest I do
not see how one can improve upon such advice ; certainly it
is not advisable to extract from the brood chamber later than
that month, and the substituted food can hardly be given too
soon, if we wish the bees to settle down quietly before cool
weather comes on.   Moreover, if the food be supplied immediately after the harvest, the remaining strength of the old
workers will be utilized in storing it, and so they perform a
beneficial act to the colony before expiring, as it is desirable
they should do.

---

Many complain that the more prolific varieties use up all
the autumn stores in brood rearing, and the same bee-keepers
will tell us that if fed up in August their bees will want feeding
again by October.   But at this time stores must not be given
slowly ; all a colony requires should be supplied in one dose in
the course of two or three days.   Give nothing more, when
breeding soon ceases and the bees invariably quiet down.

---

Dear Reader, whatever the side issues may be, I need
hardly say that bees are cultivated for the production of honey.

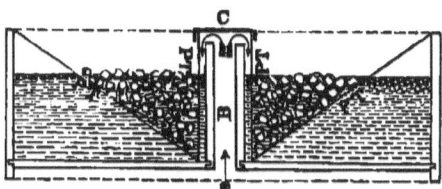

Fig. 71.
Sectional View of Simmins' Self-acting
Syrup Feeders.   (Non-cooking or cold
water process )

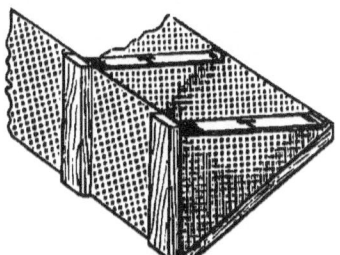

Fig. 72.
View of the Perforated Strainer
for holding sugar.

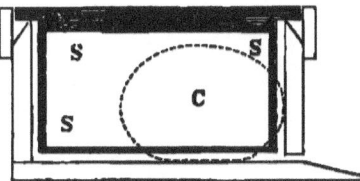

Fig. 73.
Standard Frame, shewing position
of stores and cluster at fore-part
of winter.

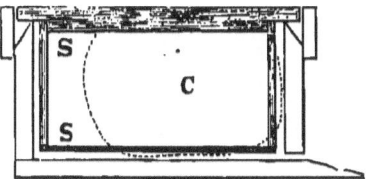

Fig. 74.
Ditto at approach of spring.

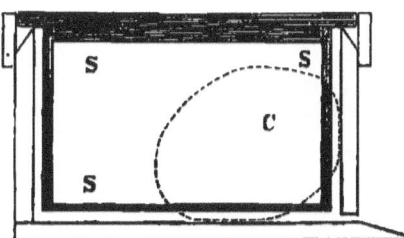

Fig. 75.
Commercial Standard, shewing position
of stores and cluster at fore-part of winter.

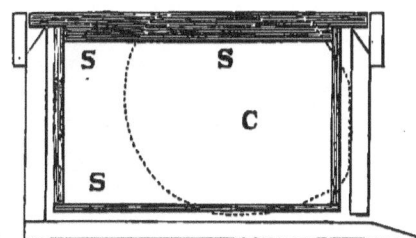

Fig. 76.
Ditto at approach of spring.

S

We have then to consider which plan of procedure will give the largest surplus with the least amount of time and capital invested. Your stock also is to be held in the highest state of excellence *generally* year after year. The desideratum to be followed is that mentioned as the " Tenth Method," which, worked together with the non-swarming system, will be found the very foundation-stone of success.

SPRING DWINDLING.—Avoid it by retaining only young queens ; let your stocks be well stored for the winter ; avoid stimulative feeding after August ; see that the combs are well stored with *pollen*. The production of young bees up to cold weather ruins the colony—such bees are of no use in wintering.

On the other hand a well found stock will not (if undisturbed) breed during October, November, and December, but with the New Year several patches of brood begin to appear, gradually increasing in size, until the full combs are occupied as the returning warmth encourages its more extensive pro- duction. All is progress, and a large youthful population is secured before the older bees take frequent flights.

Such colonies are ready for anything, and the severest cold cannot prevent the starting of brood at the centre of the cluster during January. Stocks stimulated in Autumn are those which dwindle most in Spring, because young bees are not then produced in quantity before the older workers are worn out.

Natural laws cannot be violated with impunity. The period of rest is absolutely necessary, and if that term com- mences in August better far than in November. Remember

that the earlier bees settle down, the earlier they will be in
Spring. The vital energies of a sound population have not
been wasted in producing a less hardy unseasonable batch of
youngsters, produced too at the expense of the stores of *pollen*
which were put by for early Spring use, and the absence of
which totally prevents the production of brood until a new
supply can be obtained from the fields.

Even in Summer the great and constant loss of life is
occasioned almost entirely by continued flights ; this is *the*
hard work of the bee, though frequently its wings are first to
wear, and refuse at last to carry home the body that could still.
labour. Only add the liability to chill in early Spring, and
after considering the practical relation of the foregoing facts
one has not much trouble in finding the cause of Spring
dwindling. Very late storage of a heavy crop is on a par
with late Autumn " tinkering " with bees.

It has sometimes been stated that by depriving a colony of
its queen during a honey flow a much larger harvest will be
secured. Quite true ; if one can always depend upon a heavy
flow following her removal ; but what is to compensate for the
wear and tear during the six weeks, more or less, when no
young bees are coming forward to take the place of those worn
out ? There is no compensation, and when a queen is given,
these old bees will not raise enough young ones to go through
the winter. The additional surplus, therefore, does not pay
for the total loss of stock.

To be in the highest degree profitable, year after year, a
colony must *always* be in possession of a good queen. Hitherto
it has been considered that a queen is at her best during her

second season ; but in the future, the apiarist who wishes to compete with the times will give his stock a young queen *every year.* Such young queen is not to be inserted either in the spring or usual swarming time ; but by observing the " Tenth Method " it will be seen that the whole matter is reduced to a system.

---

Systematic management is the corner-stone of successful bee-keeping. Plans and methods may be well in themselves, but unless carried out at the right time with due regard to what has preceded or may follow a certain manipulation, they are like broken links in a chain ; bringing only disaster where success should have been attained.

---

I have found bees working two and three miles away from home in good weather, but when there has been nothing nearer little or no surplus would be stored. In the best of weather stores accumulate slowly, and at great expense of life if the bees have to go more than one mile ; but with a sea of bloom within half-a-mile or less, honey almost pours into the hive ; hence the necessity of planting large crops to come on in succession near the apiary—the only course that will give a certain income year after year.

---

SYRUP WITHOUT COOKING.—American bee-keepers are just now enquiring for the best means of feeding bees with syrup without the trouble of cooking the sugar. A cold process, or self-acting principle, was introduced by me some ten years since, was illustrated in my Non-Swarming Pamphlet, and described under three forms: (1) The " Amateur," all metal and circular, holding 9 lbs., for top of the hive ; (2) The " Frame " feeder, all wood, except perforated sugar holder inside, holding about the same quantity ; and (3) The " Commercial," a double compartment feeder of full size, to go on top of the hive, and holding anything from 20 to 40 lbs. of syrup; all arranged for the simple process of putting in the usual proportions of sugar and water, when with no further attention the whole is shortly reduced to syrup.

---

The sugar must be *suspended* in the water by means of the perforated compartments as shown in Figs. 50, 52, 53, 69, 70, 71, and 72; thus allowing a free circulation of liquid under.

---

I have frequently used a large cylinder, holding nearly 2 cwt., constructed in a manner similar to the feeding-can arrangement, Fig. 52, except that a treacle valve at bottom was provided for drawing off.

---

It is only when we come to consider the immense saving of time and labour in connection with this method of syrup making, as also the plan of feeding dry sugar (Fig. 11), that one sees the possibility of conducting out-apiaries to the greatest advantage.

---

THE WINTER CLUSTER will generally be seen located towards one or other of the outside walls at the ends of the frames, and starting from near the floor at the commencement of cold weather will be found to slowly advance upwards as the stores are consumed close at hand. The illustration, as represented in Figs. 73-76, will shew clearly enough that the cluster is formed upon the empty cells wherefrom the later batches of brood were hatched, and it is at once evident the larger frame shews decided advantages in that an abundance of food is present on each frame occupied by the bees, thus ensuring that restfulness so necessary for the well-being of our little friends, and avoiding the too frequent occurrence of starvation while the distant (smaller) frames may be well stored.

The situation of the cluster is represented [by the letter C]; the stores by **S**.

It should not be forgotten that before the quilt frame covering came into use most hives were constructed with a bee-space between the frame bars and the crown-board. When the close-fitting quilt was adopted this space was closed, to the detriment of the bees, in that the cluster could no longer communicate at the spot most favorable for the purpose; consequently the outer seams of bees frequently perished.

This trouble can always be avoided by placing one or two ½-inch strips of wood at right angles to the frames, and between them and the quilt. Candy, when necessary, will do the same; so also will an additional shallow story placed above; and this latter will ever be found to give very desirable results.

THICK TOP BARS.—Just note the ⅞-inch top bar, the thickness used in my apiaries since 1878. They do not sag at the centre; do away almost entirely with comb attachments above; and help to keep the queen from ascending to the supers.

INVERSION OF THE BROOD COMBS.—About the year 1875 British bee-keepers were exercising their minds over the supposed advantages of inversion; but nothing of value was found in the practice. Ten years later the same idea cropped up in America. Now what do we hear of it?

From my Non-Swarming Pamphlet (1886) I quote the following statement I then made in reference thereto : " Much stress has been laid upon the fact that an American bee-keeper, who also is a supply dealer, has made and used several thousand reversible frames. Having taken such a stride, of course he would do all he could to maintain his position. But in a short time his 5,000 or more of such frames will, like all others now in use, remain unreversed, or will be entirely thrown aside."

QUEEN EXCLUDERS.—After expressing my own adverse opinion of the article it is only right I should tell you of the very best queen excluder it will ever be in your power to obtain. There is no patent on it, and it costs nothing. It has been shewn up over and over again throughout these pages, and yet, perhaps, you have arrived so far without grasping the situation. I do not offer a substitute for queen excluder zinc; that in itself is but a sorry substitute for the correct method of working, and the article has come into use simply because so many will not comprehend the exact state of affairs. Unite, or carry out the system of doubling, at the right time, and your bees will conduct the excluding business right enough ; they will save the expense and inconvenience of the zinc, and give you larger profits into the bargain !

EGGS DELAYED IN HATCHING.—It does not follow because eggs are deposited in the cells that the warmth of the hive must hatch them. Such is far from being the case ; no eggs will hatch until the workers first surround them with the pre-paratory food upon which the tiny grub is to feed.

Consequently, in spring, eggs laid in drone cells are some-times not brought to the hatching point for days or weeks after the usual three days period. There they remain just as deposited by the queen, and as soon as favorable weather appears the food is supplied and they are allowed to hatch.

Eggs that should produce workers are sometimes held over in this way in early spring ; but more frequently it happens with these in late autumn.

SWARMING V. HONEY.—The apiarist who is presumably working simply for honey must not only rigidly repress all natural swarming but will be compelled to double up, or unite at least two colonies into one, at the commencement of the season if he has the least hope of securing a heavy paying crop.

It is useless to attempt to *rely* upon any one apparently strong colony. The *certainty* must be attained at one stroke, and the act of doubling at the right time will enable him to secure enormous crops.

The individual stock is too frequently relied upon, only for the bee-keeper to find that the season is too far gone before earnest work is really commenced.

PURE V. CROSS-BREEDS.—One of the greatest mistakes the honey-producer can make is to attempt to secure the highest profitable results from any known *pure* race of bees.

The foreign varieties are of value almost solely as a means of improving our stock by maintaining that high state of vigour and excellence which always follows judicious crossing.

An important development in the economical production of honey, upon which I have been working for ten years past, promises at last to be a decided success; but as I must wait for a full trial during the coming season, I regret that I can not give particulars in the present edition of this work.

WELLS' SYSTEM.—It is among the most likely of possibilities that three years hence this plan will be a thing of the past. We have only to look at the higher results obtained from single hives to see that greater economy is secured all round by the use of one queen only to each working stock.

WIDE OR CLOSE-END FRAMES have been through various experiments under my hands since '75, and in '78 I was awarded a Special Prize for a hive of this class at South Kensington. The original block is as Fig. 68, and the main features were that the frames could be inverted as a whole; they had an inner side rail, while the outer ends were put on in reverse position so that the combs could lay close against the cage of the extractor. Another point was the arrangement of a crate of sections *under* the brood chamber, such as the Conqueror hive now has situated in a more convenient manner for working.

Quinby had great success with wide or close-end frames; Capt. Hetherington, one of the largest bee-keepers in America, uses them exclusively; and besides others, we have Mr. Heddon with his shallow chambers unknowingly following the character of the far-famed Stewarton horizontally divided brood chambers.

With these frames the great disadvantage has been not so much the actual contact of the frames as the fact that screws or springs were necessary to keep all up close together to avoid the trouble caused by the contraction or expansion of the wood. So much for the past; we await the developments of the future.

Metal ends for keeping brood frames equi-distant are as illustrated at Fig. 65. These were the invention of Mr. W. B. Carr, and are so cheaply produced by the well-known manufacturer, Mr. W. P. Meadows, that the cast metal ends have been driven out of the field. Their formation permits of using frames at two distinct distances from centre to centre, though the fact is seldom taken advantage of, and when once placed on the frames the set distance is retained.

FERTILIZATION OF QUEEN BEES IN CONFINEMENT!—Ah! here is one wished-for attainment which appears never likely to be accomplished. My experiments in this direction only convince me that the task is hopeless, as the drone and queen must have a full and vigorous exciting flight just prior to the act of copulation.

ARTIFICIAL HEAT!—What numerous and costly experiments have I not conducted in this direction, extending over the last ten or twelve years? It is both a destructive and a helpful process. Hurtful if applied before warm weather is really near at hand; greatly beneficial if used in a proper manner, only after the bees have once hatched plenty of young.

Greenhouses, coal-stoves, paraffin stoves and lamps; all of these have I brought into requisition, and in the light of past results all are condemned.

---

A joyous sight though it was to an enthusiast to stand in summer heat at mid-winter and watch the hundreds of busy workers at the artificial pollen, and rushing with their loads to the hives as though they made sure summer was upon them.

---

But judged by the stern light of facts it remained a pleasant experiment only, for of what value were those stocks after the excessive unseasonable loss of life and consequent failure to pick up when the second and real summer approached?

---

And yet artificial heat gave me some of the most forward stocks I ever possessed—they were up strongly in the supers by the end of April. But it was not until March was well on the way that they were placed upon and carefully packed round with long stable manure. They did well right along, and being almost exempt from all outside changes there was nothing to hinder their very rapid progress.

---

While I am not an advocate of double packed walls in winter, nor such arrangement even for summer, yet where *shade* is provided by an independent outer case during hot weather, very great progress is made by the bees.

---

Mr. Cheshire has repeatedly pointed out that queens should be reared artificially instead of using those raised under the swarming impulse, if we wish to diminish the inclination to swarm. But I go a step farther and breed from queens that have not swarmed, and whose parent and grand-- parent also had neither of them swarmed. Thus only can a non-swarming race be secured; and in this manner I have raised Carniolans, so that the excessive swarming frequently attributed to them has been quite unknown in my apiaries.

---

The English Journals devoted to Bee-culture are the *British Bee Journal* and *Beekeeper's Record*, both of which are published at 17, King William Street, Strand, London. The most prominent in America are *The American Bee Journal*, 199, Randolph Street, Chicago; *Gleanings in Bee Culture*, Medina,. Ohio; *The Review*, Flint, Michigan; *Apiculturist*, Wenham, Mass.; and *The Canadian Bee Journal*, Beeton, Ontario.

---

Dear Reader, as a parting sentence, allow me to remind you that bee-keeping cannot be carried on extensively by everyone. Success is not to be attained except by diligent study and hard work. The earnest and enthusiastic worker will find the pursuit give a reliable income if he will strive to keep only young queens bred from stock showing persistent good qualities; while additional security is offered where planting can be carried out in a systematic manner. I trust that herein you have found that I do not merely give you the usual and well-nigh worn-out advice, "Keep your stocks strong"; but instead of then leaving you to find out for yourself how it is done, I have placed before you the means, that will enable you to attain the desired end.

FINIS.

# INDEX.

T

# The "CONQUEROR"

## IMPROVED

# NON-SWARMING HIVE AND SYSTEM.

*A Surrey Beekeeper, writing February 29th, 1892, says—*

"C—., my bee-friend, remarked he never saw Hives so strong in Bees, and in such good condition at this time of the year." (**Hives and Bees supplied by us.**)

ABERCROMBIE MANSE, ST. MONANS,

*January 17th,* 1893.

"It gives me pleasure to say a word in favor of your Conqueror Hive. It has various good features. (1) No bees are crushed in the manipulation of the different parts. (2) The floor-board and all other parts can be much more easily kept clean than any other hive I know. (3) I have found your plan for preventing swarming quite successful. (4) The arrangement for obtaining honey in the supers is excellent and I have obtained more honey from the "Conqueror" than from any of my other hives. . . . The thin sides (of outer case, then only $\frac{3}{8}$ now made of $\frac{1}{2}$in. stuff) are quite sufficient for the coldest winter or the hottest summer. . . In Autumn my stock (in Conqueror) was in first rate condition, and I have no doubt that in Spring it will again be my best."

(REV.) "J. TURNBULL."

# S. SIMMINS,

# THE SOUTHERN APIARIES,

# SEAFORD, SUSSEX.

# STOCKS, SWARMS, QUEENS, NUCLEI,

## WITH OR WITHOUT HIVES.

The Season of 1892 will long be remembered by the Beekeepers of the North as the cold, stormy, and almost honeyless season. Many had to feed all through, or simply let their Bees die. And yet where other Bees did nothing, in the same apiary Bees received from us starting as mere nuclei in June were the only ones to store a surplus.

"STANLEY, N.B.,
"*July 25th*, 1892.

" You will remember I got from you 4 lots—2 Carniolan and 2 Ligurian, beginning of last July—on 6 frames each. Last season was extremely bad ; I sent all my bees to heather, and those I got from you were the only ones that came home heavier than when sent. . I sold one Carniolan and one Ligurian. . . . My Carniolan swarmed on the 26th May (the first and earliest in this district). The ' top ' swarm has a super of 21, the sections all but finished, and a super below full of Bees (for heather).

" The Ligurians have not swarmed, but are on two supers, one of them finished, the other nearly so.

" D. FENTON."

"COALBROOKDALE, SHROPSHIRE,
"*August 24th*, 1892.

" The Black crossed with Carniolan I had from you last August has broken the record here—51lbs from super, "such slabs of Honey," with several pounds left in brood chamber.

" W. MARSHALL."

"EPNEY, STONEHOUSE, GLOS.,
"*September 30th*, 1892.

"I had two queens from you two years ago; they have done well, and have been my best this season. Would like the same again (a Cyprian-cross) if you have such to part with.

"O. KNIGHT."

"TANRAGO, BALLISODARE, IRELAND,
"*August 20th*, 1892.

"The four nuclei (sent May 23rd) have done well. I had a swarm from each, and one has given some surplus besides. Your Bees are wonderful breeders and good tempered.

"R. J. V."

## S. SIMMINS,

### The Southern Apiaries, SEAFORD, SUSSEX.